MANKIW EDITION ECONOMICS:

HITS.on the Web

PART I

World Wide Web Overview
by

Carol Lea Clark
University of Texas, El Paso

Internet Activities for
Principles of Economics
prepared by

Robert S. Rycroft
Mary Washington College

URLs prepared by

Michael R. Dowd
University of Toledo

THOMSON
CUSTOM PUBLISHING

Editor: Michele Baird
Pre-Press Coordinator: Christina Smith
Production Coordinator: Brian Schaefer
Marketing Manager: Sara Hinckley

Printed in the United States of America

Thomson Custom Publishing
5191 Natorp Blvd.
Mason, Ohio 45040
USA

For information about our products, contact us:
1-800-355-9983
http://www.thomsoncustom.com

International Headquarters
Thomson Learning
International Division
290 Harbor Drive, 2nd Floor
Stamford, CT 06902-7477
USA

UK/Europe/Middle East/South Africa
Thomson Learning
Berkshire House
168-173 High Holborn
London WCIV 7AA
United Kingdom

Asia
Thomson Learning
60 Albert Street, #15-01
Albert Complex
Singapore 189969

Canada
Nelson Thomson Learning
1120 Birchmount Road
Toronto, Ontario MIK 5G4
Canada

Visit us at www.thomsoncustom.com and learn more about this book and other titles published by Thomson Custom Publishing.

ISBN: 0-759-31611-2

The Adaptable Courseware Program consists of products and additions to existing Custom Publishing products that are produced from camera-ready copy. Peer review, class testing, and accuracy are primarily the responsibility of the author(s).

CONTENTS

PART I – World Wide Web Overview 1

Chapter 1 – An Introduction to the World Wide Web 3

Chapter 2 – Browsing the Web 11

Chapter 3 – Finding Information on the World Wide Web 23

Chapter 4 – Email, Email Discussion Groups, and Newsgroups 45

Chapter 5 – Documenting Internet Sources 57

Chapter 6 – Internet Activities For *Principles of Economics* 61

Appendix – Sources of Additional Information 79

PART II – Thomsonlearning.com 81

Thomson Learning Economics Website Overview 83

PART III – Economics Websites 87

HITS Hottest Economics Sites on the Web 89

Appendix – InfoTrac Quick Start Guide A-1

Activating Your Account A-4

Searching the *InfoTrac College Edition* Database A-5

PART I

World Wide Web Overview

Chapter 1
An Introduction to the World Wide Web

Chapter 2
Browsing the Web

Chapter 3
Finding Information on the World Wide Web

Chapter 4
Email, Email Discussion Groups, and Newsgroups

Chapter 5
Documenting Internet Sources

Chapter 6
Internet Activities for *Principles of Economics*

Appendix
Sources of Additional Information

C H A P T E R 1

AN INTRODUCTION TO THE WORLD WIDE WEB

The ability to navigate the World Wide Web has become a necessity for college students. Of the five million full-time students in four-year colleges in the U.S, 90% use the Internet daily, according to a *Forbes* article. The percent of students using the Internet in two-year colleges may not be quite as high, but it is increasing rapidly. Many classes have Web pages, and some professors make lecture notes and research materials available only online. Campuses, even dorms, are being wired with fiber-optic cable to make access almost effortless. Students at Drexel University in Philadelphia are at the forefront of what will probably be common in the not too distant future; because of the university's wireless network, they can connect from the dorm's lawn and the gym as well as the library. Colleges and universities that do not have state-of-the-art connections encourage students to find their own Internet connection and may offer suggestions and assistance.

Of course, administrators and professors hope their students are using all this access to work on research for their classes, and that is happening. Knowing your way around the Internet is not just a skill for research in colleges, however. Students also spend hours emailing old friends and making new ones in chat rooms. Some invest their free time playing online games, others play the stock market with their own money. The Internet has become an amazing source of new markets. According to Nielsen/NetRatings and Harris Interactive, online transactions in January 2001 were $3.8 billion. Companies also use the Internet to communicate between offices, as well as a source for research information.

Some criticize the Internet, however, saying that it is slow during peak hours and that finding information is time consuming and frustrating. Others say it is at best a source of frivolous entertainment, and, at worst, a dangerous distraction from classes and homework. These criticisms may all be merited at one time or another, but it is also true that the Internet today is a potentially unlimited store of data, too important to boycott. In addition, efforts are being made on many levels to make the Internet faster by increasing bandwidth and to make information easier to access by refining search methods.

According to Nielsen/NetRatings, in January 2001 Internet access either at home or at work reached 169 million individuals in the United States, 60% of the population. This is an increase of eight percent since October 2000. Global Reach estimates that by 2003, 774 million people worldwide will have Internet access.

The World Wide Web's colorful, graphics-studded, and user-friendly environment appeals to an increasing number of users who may have had neither the patience nor the desire to learn the intricacies of the older and less colorful network protocols that were predominant on the Internet before the Web was developed. (*Protocols* are sets of agreed-on conventions for transferring data across a network.) But the advances of the Web over FTP (file transfer protocol), gopher, and other protocols are more than glitz. The Web offers increased flexibility and a range of media that enhances both the impact and the content of the information transmitted to the user. Indeed, the Web began as a project designed to provide a simple and convenient way to distribute scientific information across computer networks through hypertext. This hypertext interface was fashioned to allow researchers to present their work complete with text, pictures, charts, and illustrations within a system of links that enables the user to move logically from one text section to a related section in much the same way a text note in a book might refer the reader to a related section in another chapter. The hypertext design of the Web quickly matured into a resource with simple controls that anyone can learn to use and master quickly.

Hypertext really isn't new. Print dictionaries and encyclopedias use a rudimentary form of hypertext. The Macintosh HyperCard program and similar programs for Microsoft Windows use hypertext, enabling users to select highlighted items on a computer page and move to linked documents. What is revolutionary about hypertext on the Web, however, is that you can link to a document located on a computer server on your campus and then move with equal ease to documents in Boston or Brazil. Through the World Wide Web, the world has become an interconnected web of hypertext documents.

Is the Web the Internet? No. The Internet (Net) existed long before the Web, and many of the resources on the Internet are still stored in non-hypertext formats for use with older protocols, such as gopher and FTP. The Internet also includes electronic mail (e-mail) and Usenet newsgroups, a collection of some 40,000 discussion groups, which really aren't part of the Web. You can, however, access these non-Web parts of the Internet through a *browser*, a program used to navigate the Web, though they will not be in hypertext.

A Very Brief History of the Internet

The Internet long predates the World Wide Web. It began in the early 1960s as a computer communication network the U.S. military designed to survive a nuclear attack. Because it was decentralized, if one or more portions of the network had been destroyed, the others still could have communicated with each other. The original network was called ARPAnet (Advanced Research Projects Agency). Other networks followed as scientists and researchers discovered the many benefits of communicating with each other. University local area networks and, recently, commercial online services such as America Online and CompuServe have become part of the Internet. The most popular use of the Internet by far has been electronic mail, allowing people to communicate with each other around the world. The World Wide Web, however, with its colorful, user-friendly interface, is attracting millions of new users to the system.

The Internet has no central control. For many years, the acceptable-use policy dictated by the National Science Foundation, a major funding source, restricted the Internet to educational and nonprofit usage. In recent years, however, funding of the Internet has changed and commercial use has grown rapidly.

For a moment, think of what you know about how cable television works. The physical pieces of the Internet can be compared to all the cable and control equipment the cable company provides. The information stored throughout the Internet can be compared to the shows you receive through the cable system. A World Wide Web browser is analogous to the television. It gives you a convenient, easy-to-use interface for all the rich resources on the Internet in much the same way a good television provides you with an easy-to-use interface for viewing your favorite shows. Different television models and brands all provide the same function, though older ones may be in black and white rather than color; similarly, different Web browsers (and different, updated versions of Web browsers) vary in sophistication from text-only to full graphical capabilities. All the browsers, from text-only Lynx to graphical Netscape, access the same information on the World Wide Web. Even cell phones and PDAs with wireless Internet access derive their information from the same Web pages, though the pages have been reformatted to display only parts of their content on the smaller screens.

The Web's Special Characteristics

Until relatively recently, few ventured into cyberspace unless they were die-hard computer enthusiasts, educators, or scientists. The Internet had the appeal of access to huge amounts of information; before the Web, however, the Internet was unadorned and colorless, requiring the use of cryptic command prompts and menus to locate and retrieve information. The Web is a distinct improvement over earlier Internet protocols and interfaces in several important ways:

HYPERTEXT—Key words or points in one document link seamlessly with parts of other documents, whether the documents are stored on the same computer or on separate machines in distant places around the world.

HYPERMEDIA—Web pages look more like slick magazines pages than the text-only offerings of earlier Internet documents. Photos, video, sound, and interactive viewer-to-site communication make many new types of communication possible.

BROWSERS—Programs called browsers display hypertext files and allow the user, with the click of a mouse, to connect to a document and display it. To explore the Web, a user can pick an entry point (such as a university home page) and jump from one site to another, browsing at will. These programs effectively turn cyberspace into what seems like an immense disk drive.

PLUG-IN PROGRAMS—Browsers launch plug-in or auxiliary programs, which display image, sound, and video files. This keeps the size of the browser programs smaller and increases flexibility by enabling browsers quickly to support media as they become available.

ACCESS TO DOCUMENTS IN OTHER FORMATS—The Web also supports connections to documents formatted for transmission via FTP, gopher, WAIS (Wide-Area Information Server), and Usenet newsgroups, making it possible to navigate all of cyberspace without leaving a WWW browser program.

INTERACTIVITY—Many Web documents have built-in interactivity through forms that solicit responses from readers, and many Web documents include connections to Web page authors' e-mail addresses.

SELF-PUBLISHING—For the first time in publishing history, individuals have the capability of publishing documents thousands or even millions may read. All that is required for publishing is a fairly modest knowledge of *HTML* (Hypertext Markup Language) or one of a number of HTML editing programs and access to space on a server (a computer that stores Web documents).

Hypertext Transfer Protocol

Hypertext Transfer Protocol (HTTP) is the backbone of the World Wide Web. It is a series of agreed-on conventions and interlocking programs that

A Very Brief History of the World Wide Web

The Web dates back only to 1990. Based on a proposal by Tim Berner-Lee for enhancing the Internet, CERN (the European Particle Physics Laboratory in Geneva) began work on a hypertext browser. The purpose was to allow researchers to collaborate by presenting research information not only in plain text but also in hypertext with graphics, illustrations, and, eventually, sound and video. By January 1993, fifty Web servers (or computer sites offering files in Web format) existed. That same year the first version of an advanced Web browser called Mosiac was developed by Marc Andreesen at the National Center for Supercomputing Applications (NCSA) in Champaign, Illinois; because of Mosaic's user-friendly interface, interest in the Web began to spread far beyond the scientific community. By 1994, more than ten thousand servers operated, and the Web began to attract media attention, with articles appearing in the *New York Times* and other major newspapers.

make up the Web. Because HTTP is a client-server protocol, you as a user have a *client* program on your computer that uses HTTP to communicate with a remote *server* computer storing information. The remote computer runs the server portion of the Hypertext Transfer Protocol. Every document on the Web has an address (something like http://www.somewhere.edu). When you type in a World Wide Web address or click on a hypertext link, your HTTP client program (also called a browser) attempts to connect to the remote computer you have requested. The address you give your browser also has the name of a file or, by default, the home page file. When a connection to the remote computer is established, the server looks for the file and, if it is found, downloads it to your computer. If the file isn't found, you receive an error message. Once the file downloads from the server, your client program takes over and displays the file according to its format, which may be hypertext, graphics, sound, video, or something else.

Hypertext Markup Language

Hypertext Markup Language (HTML) is a system of codes embedded in text documents that tells a Web client (browser) program how to display the document as hypertext. The codes indicate links to other documents, placement of graphics, headings, alignments, and so on. You don't need to master HTML unless you want to create Web documents yourself. If you simply want to explore the Web and use its resources, your browser program reads and interprets the codes for you.

APPLICATIONS OF THE WORLD WIDE WEB

The Web has become a repository for endless amounts of information on almost any subject imaginable. For example, in Thomas (http://thomas.loc.gov), the site for the United States Congress, you can read or download the full text of pending legislation and check on the status of bills. Because the Web can be updated so quickly, it is also an excellent source for information that changes quickly, such as stock quotes or weather conditions. The chapters that follow in this book explain how to research topics, discuss major research resources, and offer a list of subject-specific Websites in your discipline.

The World Wide Web is a reflection of world culture. It's a quirky and inconsistent mix of serious research, commercial promotion, entertainment, individual opinions, propaganda, and any other type of communication humans can invent. Much out there is valuable; some of it you may consider worthless, and other things may amuse you. Certainly no one person can absorb all the sites; what you can learn are techniques that help you to find what you want to find, whether it be serious research or recreation.

Accessing the World Wide Web via Colleges and Universities

To access the Web, you must have an Internet connection and a browser program, so named because it allows you to browse or explore the Web. If you are a student in a college or university, you may have free or low-cost access to the World Wide Web and the Internet. Likely, you will connect to the Web in one of the following ways:

- Through computer labs with full graphical browsers such as Internet Explorer or Netscape Navigator installed.
- By telephone modem access from home provided by your college or university. With this type of connection, you can use Internet Explorer or another graphical browser from your home computer. If your university offers this type of access, it also should provide you with instructions on how to implement it.
- Computer labs or dial-up modem access with text-only World Wide Web capability. Some universities use Lynx or another text-only browser, which enables you to access the text portions of the World Wide Web but not the graphics, sound, or video. Commonly, Lynx is accessed from a menu-based shell system. Ask at the computer help desk at your university. They can explain how to access the menu either in the university labs or by dial-up remote connection.

Other Options for Access

- Commercial online services such as America Online (AOL) and the Microsoft Network now provide telephone modem connections to the World Wide Web. Most offer free introductory hours to try their services. Then you pay a flat fee per month. These providers may also offer additional services, such as chat rooms (electronic discussions) or research materials that are not part of the Internet.
- Internet service providers, either local or national companies, offer SLIP or PPP full Internet access, including e-mail and other Internet protocols in addition to the World Wide Web. They generally offer no additional services that are not part of the Internet. These providers may also supply you with software and instructions for installation. Their fees may be lower than commercial online services.
- Many cable television companies now offer high-speed modem access via a cable connection. A cable modem is an external devices that connect to a network card installed in your computer. Like other commercial online services, they may offer additional services to their subscribers. An advantage of cable access is that it does not tie up a telephone line while you use the Internet.
- DSL (Digital Subscriber Line) is a relatively new trend in high-speed Internet access. DSL works over existing copper telephone lines and is typically offered by telephone companies. DSL uses a different part of the frequency spectrum than analog voice signals, so it can work in conjunction with your standard analog telephone service, sharing the same pair of wires.

CHAPTER 2

BROWSING THE WEB

The ideal way to browse the World Wide Web is to have the most recent version of a full-graphical browser such as Internet Explorer or Netscape Navigator, running on a fast computer with a fast Internet connection; together these enable you to appreciate all the graphics and sound available on the Web and to explore links with a simple click of the mouse.

Alternatively, an increasing number of users are finding that access to the Internet can be mobile and wireless. Some are using laptop computers with modems. Others, wanting even more portability, are accessing the Web through devices such as Personal Digital Assistants (also called PDAs or handhelds) or cellular telephones.

Some users, however, find they are, at least for the present, restricted to a less-than-optimal connection to the Internet. They may not have access to a full-featured browser, either because of limitations of the computers or of the networks they are using. They are thus restricted to text-only browsers which rarely support any features more advanced than simple text display and links. Still, text-only browsers are available and enable such users to consider important information on the Web.

Internet Explorer and Netscape Navigator are the most popular of the graphical browsers, though specialized browsers still hold their own places on the Net. Internet Explorer and Netscape are used in this book to demonstrate navigating the Web. If you are using another graphics-oriented browser, however, your commands will be similar.

BROWSWERS

Client–Server Model

The World Wide Web uses a client-server model. A Web browser is a client program that runs on your computer. When you give instructions to the client program through keystrokes or clicks of a mouse, the client program requests information from a remote computer running a server program. Most obviously, you might instruct that a Web page be downloaded to your computer. A *server* is a computer that stores Web pages, and the *server program* sends the data to your *client* browser program. In general, you need only know how the client part of the client-server model works, and this chapter is about that.

Anatomy of a Web Address

All documents on the World Wide Web have specific addresses called URLs (Universal Resource Locators). A Web address may look something like this:

http://www.mtv.com

Or you may see a variation like **www.mtv.com** without the prefix http://, or even **mtv.com**. These addresses are domain names, or nickname addresses, which are a variation of the organization name and, thus, memorable. Other examples would include http://www.whitehouse.gov, the address for the White House, or http://www.microsoft.com, the address for Microsoft Corporation. Technically, http://www.mtv.com is the correct way to write the Web address for the MTV home page, but recent versions of browsers will also accept **www.mtv.com** or **mtv.com**.

Other Web page addresses may look like this:

http://computer.institution.edu/filename.html

In this URL, the http stands for *hypertext transfer protocol*, a designation that tells the browser program that the document you are requesting is in hypertext format. Next comes the ://, which are simply symbols indicating that an address follows. Next are the name of the computer where the document is housed, a designation of the institution, and the suffix .edu, indicating an educational institution. Other suffixes for Web locations follow:

.com (commercial)

.edu (educational)

.gov (government)

.mil (military)

.net (networking, also used for commercial)

.org (noncommercial)

Addresses also may indicate the country of origin outside the United States. These are, for example,

.jp (Japan)

.uk (United Kingdom)

.nl (The Netherlands)

.ca (Canada)

After the slash mark is the specific document or file name and the .html (or htm) notation, which indicates the file is in *Hypertext Markup Language*, the language used to create hypertext documents.

The Internet Explorer Screen has navigational buttons and pull-down menus across the top and a box at the bottom where Web pages are displayed.

Accessing a Browser Program

If you are using a computer in one of your university's labs, chances are that Internet Explorer or Netscape is installed, and you can launch it by clicking on the browser's icon on your screen or by selecting it from the *Start* button. Your university or college may offer a dial-up connection which allows you to use a browser installed on your computer at home. Many colleges and universities, however, expect students to find their own Internet connections. If that is the case, consult "Other Options for Access" in Chapter 1.

Accessing Internet Explorer or Netscape will call up the browser window, which consists of several menus above the space where Web pages appear.

Essentials for Using the Browser

To begin navigating the Web using a browser, you need to understand only a few basics:

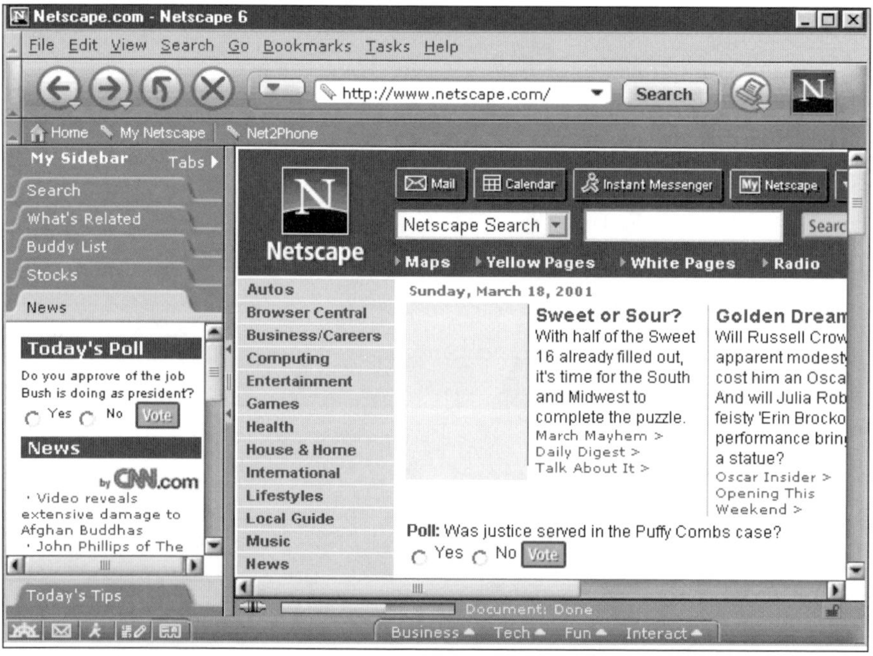

Netscape also offers buttons and pull-down menus for navigating Web pages which appear in the box at the bottom of the screen.

1. From any Web page, you can connect to other Websites by clicking on hypertext links, which are often graphics or photos. Other links may be words that are highlighted and sometimes underlined. It is easy to tell what is a hypertext link (also called a *hot link*), and what is not, by moving the cursor over the word or image. If your cursor turns into a handprint and a Web page address appears at the lower border of the browser, that word or image is a hot link to another page. If you move to a new Web page by clicking on a hypertext link, you can return to your previous page by clicking the *Back* button. You also can move forward to a previously viewed page by clicking on the *Forward* button. Thus, you can navigate throughout the Web by using these two buttons, *Back* and *Forward*.
2. If you know a World Wide Web address and want to connect directly to it, you can do so with either Internet Explorer or Netscape in two ways:
   - ✦ Select *Open* or *Open page* from the *File* pull-down menu, and a dialog box will open. You then can enter the address. Click on *Open* or *Okay* (depending on the browser) in the dialog box, and the browser will connect you to the page represented by that address.
   - ✦ Use the *Address* window near the top of the browser screen to connect to a Web address. Simply highlight the address in the box, begin to type in the desired address (this will delete the previous address), and touch *Enter*. In Internet Explorer, if you don't know the complete address, type part of the address or name of a site, type it into the Address bar, and you'll get a list of possible sites similar to what you typed.
3. A Web page can be of any length, though most are longer than what can be displayed in the box on the computer screen. Use the scroll bar at the right side of the screen to move up and down in a page.
4. Watch the icon in the upper right corner of the browser screen. If the logo is animated, then a transfer is in progress. Note the progress bar at the lower left corner of the page. As a page loads, numbers appear here that show the percentage of the page already downloaded. If the logo is not animated, then your connection is stalled.
5. If you are connecting to a site and it is taking a long time to connect, you may have tried to connect to a location experiencing technical problems. Click on the *Stop* button to abort the attempted connection. Then you can try the connection again or try a different address.

Major Browser Options

PRINT	Click on the Print button or use the *File* menu and select Print.

SAVE	Under the *File* menu, select *Save as*, and you can save the current Web page on a disk or on your hard drive. You have the option of saving as either a text file or an HTML file.
SEARCH	Chick on the *Search* button to receive a page of links to Web search engines. You can enter a key word in one of the search engines, and it will return a list of sites that relate to that topic.
HISTORY	Click the *History* button in Internet Explorer, and you will see a list of sites you have visited recently. Netscape has a similar function, but it is under the *Go* menu at the top of the screen.

NAVIGATING WITH INTERNET EXPLORER

Internet Explorer is loaded ready-to-use in most new PC computers. Each succeeding version of Internet Explorer has new features. For example, Internet

INTERNET EXPLORER'S TOOLBAR BUTTONS

Across the top of the Internet Explorer screen is a series of toolbar buttons that activate features you will use frequently in Internet Explorer.

These are their functions:

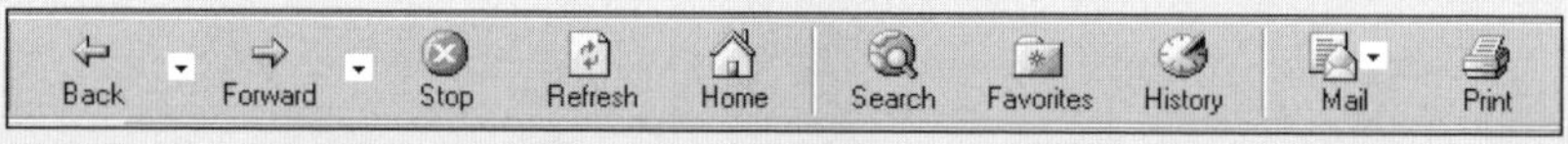

Back	Takes you back a page.
Forward	Takes you forward to a previously viewed page.
Stop	Stops the loading of a Web page.
Refresh	Reloads the current page.
Home	Takes you to the default home page for Explorer or to one you have selected.
Search	Links to a search page displaying Web search engines. Internet Explorer 5.5 allows you to specify what type of search you want to do, and Internet Explorer will choose a search service for that type of request.
Favorites	Connects to your list of favorite Websites.
History	Displays a list of Websites you viewed recently. By default, the History bar organizes Web pages in folders by week, then by day. You can choose other options, however. You can, for example, view the history list by pages you visit most often or arranged in alphabetical order.
Mail	Accesses Explorer's mail program.
Print	Prints the Web page.

Explorer 5.5 has an AutoComplete feature. It allows you to type a partial Web address in the Address bar, and a list of potential matches appears. If you've accessed that Web address before, you can simply click on the match and not have to type in the complete address. Another improvement you may find useful in Internet Explorer 5.5 is the ability to preview Web pages exactly as they will appear when printed.

You can download the most recent version from Internet Explorer's home page, http://www.microsoft.com/windows/ie. Version 5.5 requires 486DX/66 MHz or higher processor and Windows 95, Windows 98, or Windows NT 4.0. For Windows 95 and Windows 98, it requires a minimum of 16 MB (megabytes) of RAM, and for Windows NT it requires a minimum of 32 MB of RAM.

The purposes of Internet Explorer's primary buttons and menus are outlined in the following boxes, and Internet Explorer also offers help screens that have additional documentation.

Navigating with Netscape

Netscape is a preferred choice for some users. If your computer is a fairly new one, it came with Internet Explorer already installed. If you decide to

Internet Explorer's Primary Menus

Across the top of the screen above the buttons is a series of pull-down menus that enable you to take advantage of many of Internet Explorer's features.

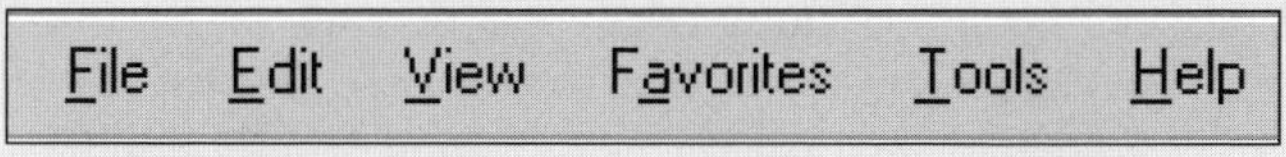

Briefly, the menus have these and other functions:

File	Offers connection to many of the main browser functions, some of which also have buttons, such as *open* (for opening the Website), *save* (to save a Web page), *print*, and *close*
Edit	Allows you to save all or a portion of the text content of a Web page
View	Enables you to control the tools visible on your browser screen (such as the standard buttons and address box) and also to open a box that displays the HTML content of the current page
Favorites	Provides a connection to a list of Websites you designate as favorites; this feature may not be usable in a computer lab
Tools	Use to access mail and newsgroups
Help	Connects you to Explorer's many help screens

use Netscape Navigator, part of Netscape Communicator, you can download the latest version from the Netscape site, http://www.netscape.com. Explore the pull-down menus and buttons at the top of the Netscape page. The purpose of each is outlined in the following boxes, and Netscape itself offers documentation in help screens that can be assessed from the *Help* pull-down menu.

PLUG-INS AND WEB ACCESSORIES

Plug-ins are software programs, often created by other software companies, that run as auxiliaries to a Web browser and expand its capabilities. Real Audio, for example, is a plug-in that allows the computer to play sound files as they are downloaded to your computer.

You should have Netscape Navigator 2.0 or later, or Internet Explorer 3.0 or later, to install plug-ins. Recent versions of the browsers offer some plug-ins as part of normal installation. Internet Explorer now includes Macromedia Flash and Macromedia Shockwave Player as part of standard installation.

When you access a site, if your computer does not have the correct plug-in, a box will pop up offering you a link to a site where you can download the plug-in. Connect to the plug-in's download site, and download it just as you would any other program. If you are in a lab, the computer likely has settings that will not allow you to download additional plug-ins. If so, check with the lab assistant about how to proceed; a designated computer might have the plug-in, or the staff may be able to add it for you.

Using a plug-in is easy. Some are activated simply by accessing a Web page that requires it. With others, like RealAudio, you click on a hot link to activate the plug-in.

Web Accessories are also utilities, but their function is to allow you to customize Internet Explorer by adding toolbar buttons or Explorer bars that stay open in the browser while you surf to different Websites. For example, you can have explorer bars which provide current stock quotes or breaking news stories. If you are interested, check out the Web Accessories page which can be accessed from the Internet Explorer home page.

FAVORITES OR BOOKMARKS

One of the most useful customized features of Web browsers is the Favorites or Bookmark option, which allows you to save the names and URLs of sites on the Net you would like to access easily. In Internet Explorer, you can add a bookmark to a Web page you are viewing by going to the *Favorites* pull-down menu and selecting *Add to Favorites*. In Netscape, click the Bookmarks icon and select *Add to Bookmarks*.

NETSCAPE'S TOOLBAR MENUS

Across the top of the Netscape screen is a series of toolbar buttons that activate features you will use frequently in Netscape.

These are their functions:

Left arrow	Back to the previous page
Right arrow	Goes forward to the next page
Curved arrow	Reloads the current page
Letter X	Stops loading of the page
Search	Connects to Netscape's search page
Print	Prints document

NETSCAPE'S PRIMARY MENUS

Across the top of the screen above the buttons are a series of pull-down menus that enable you to take advantage of many of Netscape's features.

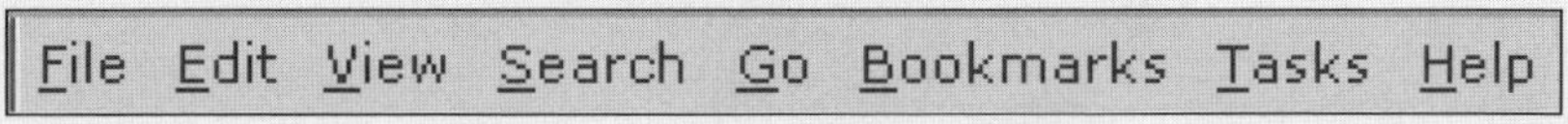

Briefly, the menus have these and other functions:

File	Accesses many features such as Open Web Page and Save Page As (save to a file on your computer).
Edit	Allows you to Copy (puts a copy of highlighted text on the clipboard), Select All (highlights everything on the current page so you can copy), and Find (finds a word in the current page).
View	Reloads the page, shows the Page Source (displays HTML codes as well as text), and provides Page Info (title, location, date of last modification).
Search	Connects to the Netscape Search page.
Go	Reviews a list of the sites you have visited in your session, which is useful if you decide you want to reexamine a site.
Bookmarks	Connects to list of sites you have marked as favorites.
Tasks	Connects to Mail and Instant Messenger.
Help	Connects to Netscape's Help screens

VIEWING PAGES OFFLINE

Internet Explorer 5.5 allows to you save pages for viewing offline which can be useful if you are not connected to the Internet at all times. You simply save a Web page to your Favorites list as usual but also check the box that specifies making the item available offline. You can also update all your favorite pages at the same time by using the *Synchronize* command on the *Tools* menu.

DEFAULT HOME PAGE

When you open a browser program, it immediately accesses a particular page. If you would like, for example, to have your browser set to connect to the *New York Times* home page, you can do so. To change to a different home page in Internet Explorer, go to the page you want, click the **Tools** menu, and then click **Internet Options**. On the **General** tab, click **Use Current**. In Netscape, go the *Edit* menu and select *Preferences*. You can then indicate your preference for a default home page.

OTHER PROTOCOLS

Some documents on the Internet are not in hypertext format. Sometimes you will find that a link from a Web page will take you to a gopher or FTP document. These documents will look different from Web documents because they do not have color or graphics. Also, you can identify them because the address displayed once you connect to them will not be a Web address. FTP and gopher sites are organized by directories or menus rather than hypertext links.

If you are using a library online catalog or connect to an interactive online text game such as a MUD or MOO, your browser may use a Telnet client to connect you to the remote computer. Telnet site commands vary, but usually a help file will instruct you on the basic commands of each site.

You may have a specific address of a document not in HTML format. You can access these through the Web by using an address designation, specifying the type of document followed by the address. These are the main file type designations:

gopher://address	telnet://address
ftp://address	news://address

Personal Digital Assistants (PDAs or Handhelds) and Cellular Telephones

At time of publication, surfing the Web with a handheld or cellular telephone may be the ultimate in Web portability, but it is vastly different than the full-graphical Web interface you have probably come to expect. What you see on a handheld or cell phone screen are Web "clippings" that are condensed text-only versions of certain Web pages that have agreed to accommodate the handheld and/or cellular telephone format. Yes, you can access stock quotes and other crucial information but certainly not everything on the Web. However, options for access are becoming more extensive all the time, with experiments such as the offering of Stephen King's "Dreamcatcher" in downloadable ebook format for PDAs.

Things to Remember

1. Web browsers such as Internet Explorer and Netscape Navigator, programs used to explore the Web, are fairly user friendly. Once you have accessed the program, you can learn its features largely by trial and error, clicking on buttons to see what they do.
2. You can use a Web browser to jump from one page to another by clicking on the hypertext links, or you can type in a specific Web address in the *Address* window and then press *Enter*.
3. Internet Explorer and Netscape offer user help. Select the *Help* pull-down menu.

C H A P T E R 3

Finding Information on the World Wide Web

The World Wide Web is an incredible resource for research. Through it, you can find full text of pending legislation, searchable online editions of Shakespeare's plays, environmental impact statements, stock quotes, and much, much more.

Finding the research sources you need, however, is not always easy. Research on the Web is far more than surfing. It involves developing a purpose for your research; making a research plan; searching using the different types of access resources, such as subject indexes, keyword search engines, online libraries, and links to magazines. It also involves evaluating the material for relevance, accuracy, and bias.

The Internet is immense, and its research materials are seemingly endless. For example, if you enter the word *environment* in one of the keyword search engines, you may receive thousands of "hits," or sites that relate to that topic from all over the world. How do you sift through all of that feedback in order to find information germane to your topic? It is a problem that hasn't been completely solved on the Internet. However, some strategies will help.

Managing Information

Define Your Purpose

As with any library research project, you need to begin by analyzing your research problem. If you are doing research for a class, your instructor may have given you the assignment in writing. Read it closely. What does your instructor ask you to do? Does he or she ask you to describe something such as environmental resources on the Internet or current treatments for AIDS patients? If so, you will be writing an *informative paper*. You will need to research the topic closely and then to summarize information related to that topic for your audience. An informative paper is more than a summary, however. You will need to focus the information in an original way that illuminates the subject for your audience.

Your assignment may ask you to argue a position or to persuade your audience to behave in a certain way. For example, you may be asked to argue for or against current practices in environmental protection. If so, you will be writing an *argumentative paper*. You will need to research your topic until you can develop a position about your topic and support that position with evidence.

Make a Research Plan

Will you be using the Internet simply as one research tool along with print texts and CD-ROM databases? For many topics, some of the most current information can be found on the Web, and it can greatly enhance your information collection. Or will you be gathering all your information from the Internet? Not all topics have equal coverage on the Internet, but for many subjects (if your instructor agrees) you can collect everything you need without leaving your computer terminal. This chapter discusses the following types of resources for locating research information on the Web.

SEARCH ENGINES—Sites that allow you to search with one or more keywords for your subject or to explore sites by topic indexes. Most search engines also have subject indexes that allow you to follow branching topical menus.

MEDIA LINKS—Sites that allow you to find full-text magazine and newspaper articles on your subject.

FULL-TEXT LIBRARY DATABASES—Your college library may offer Web access to full-text databases of magazine, journal, and newspaper articles.

LIBRARIANS' SUBJECT INDEXES—Indexes to the Web organized by topic with Websites that librarians select

When making a research plan, you need to consider your assignment. Does it say, "Write an argumentative essay about an environmental problem such as toxic waste or acid rain"? If so, you know you need to narrow the topic from the environment in general to a more specific topic such as toxic waste and perhaps to an even more specific topic such as programs for nuclear waste disposal or the recycling of environmentally damaging substances. If you aren't sure what specific topic interests you, you will need to look first at some general sources about the environment to help you choose a topic.

Several research resources on the Web can help you narrow a topic and then gather information about it.

You might, for example, examine some of the online magazines that deal with environmental topics, or you might examine the subject indexes, which might have a heading and subheadings on environmental issues. Subject indexes can be found both in search engine sites and in librarians' subject index sites. How to use these indexes will be discussed later in the chapter. Browsing these resources, you may, for example, narrow your topic to community programs for recycling.

Once you have decided on a narrow topic such as community programs for recycling, you can use the other subject indexes, keyword search engines, full-text databases, and media links to find additional resources. As you locate resources, assemble them in a working bibliography, which will help you keep track of them also as potential resources. Remember that research is a repetitive process. As you explore sources, you may find yourself changing the narrow topic you have selected, and this will require you to find additional sources. Even when you reach the writing stage of your project, you still may need to locate information sources to fill holes in your argument. The research is not complete until the project is complete.

Develop a Working Bibliography

A working bibliography for a World Wide Web research project is a list of sites and their URLs (addresses), as well as articles you may find in online

Sample Working Bibliography

Topic: Violence on Television

Linn, Susan. "Sellouts." *American Prospect.* 23 Oct 2000: 17-20. (Periodical Abstracts database)

Schroeder, Ken. "TV Teaches Violence." *Educational Digest* Sept. 1998: 74-75 (Periodical Abstracts database)

"TV Violence is pervasive..." *National Coalition on TV Violence.* <http:www.nctvv.org>

"Two New Studies on Television Violence and Their Significance for the Kids' TV Debate." The UCLA Television Violence Monitoring Report (September 1995) UCLA Center for Communication Policy and National Violence Study (February,1996) Mediascope, Inc. <http://www.cep.org/tvviolence.html>

"Violence on Television: What do Children Learn? What Can Parents Do?" American Psychological Association. <http://www.apa.org/pubinfo/violence.html>

"When Good Networks Go Bad: Rampaging animals...cheating spouses...big ratings... shockumentaries are hot!" *Time.* 1 Feb. 1999 <http://www.time.com/time/magazine/article/0,9171,19170,00.html>

RESEARCH STRATEGY FOR WORLD WIDE WEB SOURCES

1. Using a subject index (either in a search engine or a librarians' subject index), browse sites in your general topic. See what kinds of information are available on what specific topics.
2. Check online media links for articles on your general topics.
3. Search one or more of your library's full-text periodical databases for your general topic.
4. Narrow your search to a specific enough topic to write about in the length of research paper you intend to prepare.
5. Use one or more keyword search engines to locate relevant sites. Use advanced search options (described later in this section) to customize your search.
6. Compile the resources you have identified into a working bibliography. As you read through the materials available at different sites, continue to explore and record links they offer to related sites.

publications and full-text databases your library provides online. As you browse these resources, you will see many that seem relevant to a possible research project. Write down the URLs or article locations. Otherwise, if you want to return to a particular site or article, you may not remember the sequence that led you to it. The brief working bibliography below was compiled while researching violence on television.

Evaluate Your Sources

Many people tend to believe what they see in print. If information is in a book or a news magazine, it must be true. If you read critically, however, you know that all sources must be evaluated. Does a source give a balanced reporting of the evidence, or does it display bias? What resource sources are cited? What authorities? With the Internet, perhaps even more than with print texts, it is important to evaluate your sources. Undoubtedly, much reliable and valuable information is published through the Web, and you should not hesitate to use sources that, in your judgment, are credible. Remember, though, not all information on the Web is accurate. Anyone with a Web connection and a little knowledge can create a site, and automated search engines will include them in their databases. Also, many sites are commercial and may have their own marketing reasons for promoting certain information. Before relying on information, ask yourself the questions listed in "Evaluating Web Sources" below.

Evaluating Web Sources

1. Who is the sponsoring organization or individual? If no author or sponsoring organization is listed, you have no way to ascertain the document's quality.
2. If an author or sponsor is listed for the site, are any credentials offered that establish credibility? Does anything indicate that the individual/organization has expert knowledge about the topic? Does anything indicate the individual might have bias toward the topic?
3. What are the criteria for including information at the site? Are the documents collected for a stated reason? If so, does that reason enhance or detract from the apparent validity of the information?
4. If it is a business or corporate site, is its purpose marketing or sales? If so, how does that affect any content information at the site?
5. If it is a advocacy page (attempting to influence public opinion), does the organization give you an address or telephone number for verifying their legitimacy? Is it clear that the Web page has the sanction of the official organization?
6. What about the texts? Do they offer a balanced viewpoint? Do they cite sources for the evidence they offer to support their arguments?
7. Is the site technologically sophisticated? Do the graphics or other presentation elements add to or distract from the textual content?

Of course, you may be intentionally studying biased sources on the Web such as home pages of political candidates, special interest groups, or companies selling products. If so, do not take their information at face value. Indeed, you can make your evaluation of biased texts part of your argument. You could, for example, compare what a company selling a health food supplement says about that product with what you read in your search of other texts related to that product (perhaps including scientific studies). One of the Web's revolutionary aspects is that individuals and organizations can put their side of the story directly before the public. It is part of your job as a Web consumer to evaluate critically the motivation or validity of these direct-to-the-public texts.

Search Engines

The Web has a wide variety of searching tools, and more are added as the Web continues to grow. Keyword search engines are the most visible of the

SAMPLE SEARCH

Subject Index

Suppose your instructor has asked you to write an essay about an environmental issue. You don't have a clear idea about a topic and decide to explore. Connect to one of the search engines that has a subject index such as Yahoo! (http://www.yahoo.com). Examine the subject entry on the *Environment and Nature* under *Society and Culture*. You can click on any of the subtopics to receive a list of sites related to that subtopic. Or you can specify a search term in the box given for keywords (be sure also to click on the button that indicates to search only in that subcategory).

After browsing a number of the categories under environment and nature in Yahoo! (or another of the subject indexes), you may be able to narrow your topic, perhaps to recycling and then, even more specifically, to community programs for recycling.

Before you decide on a topic for your paper, however, you may want to peruse what other subject indexes have to offer because each is different. When you have a firm topic, you can try a keyword search.

YAHOO!

Categories

- Business *(13)*
- Climate Change *(58)* NEW!
- Companies@
- Conservation *(274)*
- Disasters *(151)*
- Ecology@
- Ecotourism@
- Education *(141)*
- Employment *(27)*
- Energy@
- Environment and Development Policies *(16)*
- Environmental Economics *(21)*
- Environmental Health@
- Environmental Justice *(22)*
- Environmental Psychology@
- Environmental Security *(9)*
- Environmental Studies *(79)* NEW!
- Environmentalists *(70)*
- Institutes *(81)*
- Legal Issues@
- Meteorology@
- Mining Issues@
- Mountains *(139)*
- Natural History Museums *(85)*
- Nature Centers *(296)* NEW!
- Nature Writing@
- News and Media *(161)*
- Oil and Gas Issues@
- Organizations *(3421)* NEW!
- Overpopulation@
- Ozone Depletion *(22)*
- Parks and Public Lands@
- Pollution *(204)*
- Recycling@
- Reference *(12)*
- Regional Information *(51)*
- Sustainable Development *(361)* NEW!

Explore the subtopics in a general topic category, or use the keyword search capability only in that topic category.

tools, allowing you to type in a word or words and generate a list of sites that may relate to that topic. One of the major problems with using keyword search engines for research, however, is that the number of sites and documents on almost any topic is so immense that the number of hits or potential resources located for a keyword can run into the thousands. Alternatively, for an uncommon topic, you might receive no hits at all. This problem led to the development of subject indexes, which divide Web resources into broad categories, such as education, health, and so on. Most of the general search engines also have subject indexes. All subject indexes are hierarchical, with major directories connecting to subdirectories and most also offer a keyword search mechanism within subject categories, so after you have narrowed a topic somewhat, you can type in a keyword and search in only part of the database.

Most of the keyword engines allow you to do more sophisticated searches than simply entering one or two key words. Unfortunately, the advanced search features vary widely from one engine to another. Generally, however, the engines offer a help screen that gives instructions on how to customize a search. These are some common search features:

QUOTATION MARKS—Some of the search engines allow you to put search strings in quotes, indicating that those words must appear in that order in the text. If you are looking for sites about radioactive waste, you could put the words in quotation marks "radioactive waste." Many search engines will recognize proper names, however, so you may not need to put quotation marks around *William Faulkner* if you are searching for information about that author.

PLUS AND MINUS SIGNS—Place a plus (+) in front of a word, and all hits will include that word. Place a minus (–) in front, and none of the hits will include the word.

BOOLEAN OPERATORS—You use words such as *and* and *not* to limit your search. For example, if you use the keywords *radioactive waste*, some of the search engines will return hits for either *radioactive* or *waste*. If you type *radioactive and waste*, however, the search engine will look for those two terms together. If you use the keywords *Shakespeare and not plays* you will receive hits about Shakespeare but not his plays.

Most of the general search engines give you some kind of a description with each hit, rather than just the site name and the Web address. And most return hits in order of relevancy (as perceived by an automated program). So, even if you receive a large number of hits, a few minutes spent perusing them will generally result in finding helpful sites.

Major General Search Engines

ALTAVISTA

http://www.altavista.com

This is one of the most comprehensive search engines, indexing over 250 million Web pages. Alta Vista is a full-text index that searches the entire HTML file, not just the title, and it supports both simple and advanced searches. A good standby, but not a particularly innovative search engine.

ASK JEEVES

http://www.askjeeves.com

Ask Jeeves lets you type in a real question, rather than a series of key words, and it tries to link you to a page that can answer your question. If it can't find an answer for you in its own database, it will provide Web pages from several other search engines.

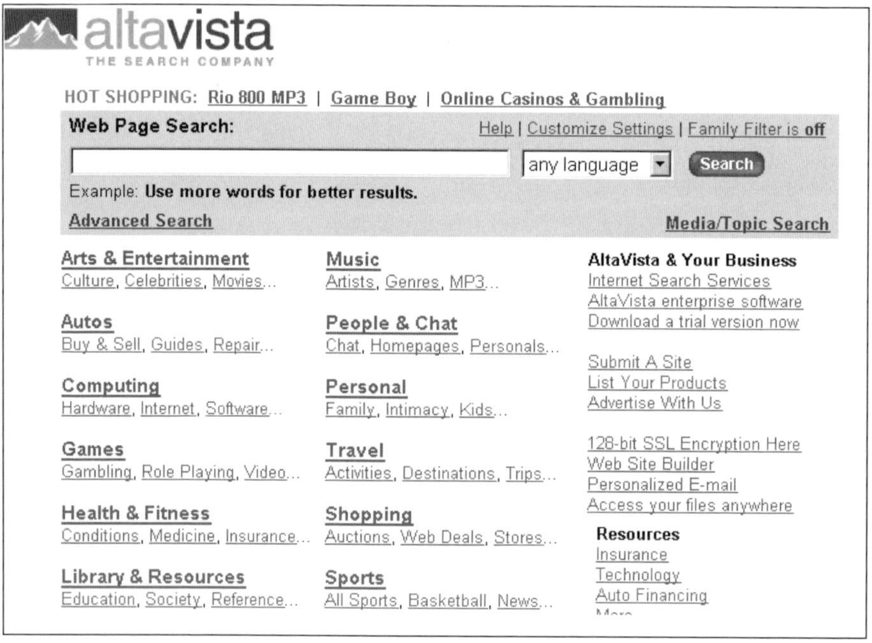

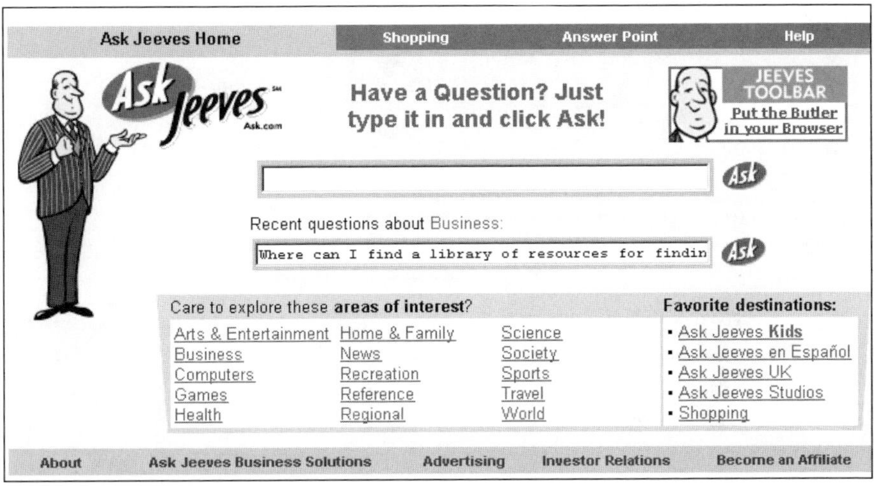

EXCITE

http://www.excite.com

Excite indexes 250 million pages and media objects, and also indexes Usenet newsgroups which can be a great resource for up-to-the-minute research. If you find a page listed on Excite that meets your research needs, you can click on a link to "find similar pages," a tool that allows you to try key words that you might not have considered for your subject.

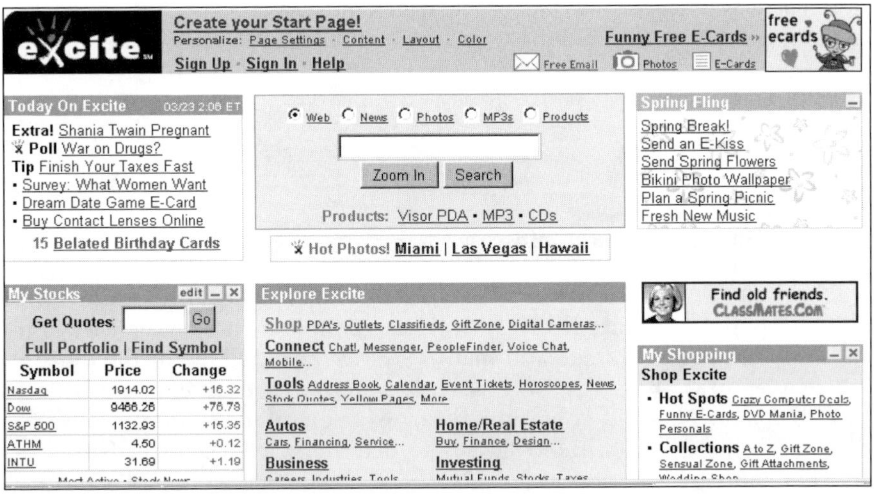

GOOGLE

http://www.google.com

This is a popular search engine which indexes some 1.25 billion web pages. It is a full-text index that searches the entire HTML file. Google has acquired a reputation for scoring hits with high relevancy. This is because it uses link popularity as a way to rank Websites, which means that users "vote" for sites by linking to them, a techniques that works well for general searches.

GO NETWORK (formerly Infoseek)

http://www.go.com

Another popular engine, Go Network, has 75 million sites and is known for its comprehensive coverage and high relevancy of hits. One of the most attractive features about the Go Network is that after each entry, it offers a link to *Similar Pages*. If you find a listing of one useful site, you can use this feature to find others without having to determine what keywords to specify. For more search options, check the welcome screen, usually the first screen you see.

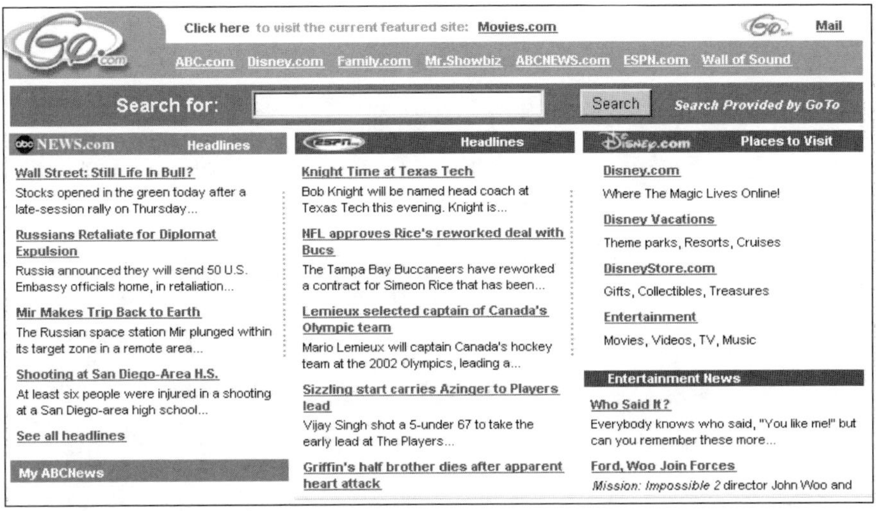

HOTBOT

http://hotbot.lycos.com

HotBot is popular with researchers because of its advanced search options. It relies upon the Open Directory Project and Inktomi databases for its listings. HotBot attempts to be highly comprehensive, and this sometimes causes a problem with deriving hits that are relevant.

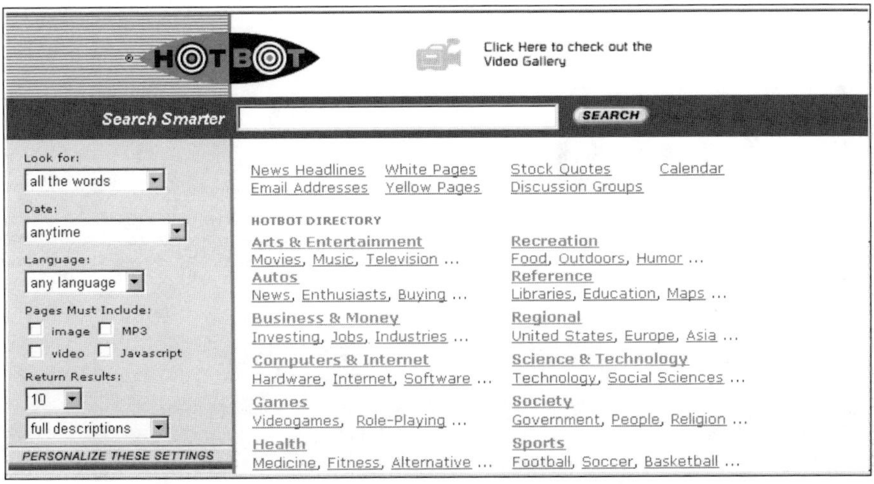

LYCOS

http://www.lycos.com

Lycos was one of the largest of the older search engines on the Web, and it has remained viable because it continues to add new features such as the subject index which is modeled on Yahoo's. Lycos is known for strong relevancy ranking capabilities, and it offers both simple and advanced searching.

OPEN DIRECTORY PROJECT

http://dmoz.org

Open Directory attempts to be the most comprehensive directory of the Web, and it has over 1.8 million listings in a easy-to-use directory format. It relies upon volunteers to catalog Websites.

YAHOO!

http://www.yahoo.com

Yahoo! remains one of the most useful and popular directories on the Web, thanks to its editors who categorize the web. Yahoo has over 1 million sites in its directories which can also be key-word searched. In addition, Yahoo uses Google to supplement its results.

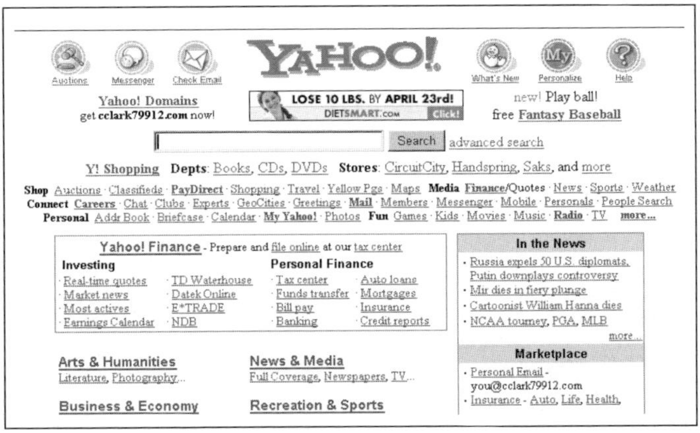

Sample Search

Keyword Search Engine

Suppose you want to write a paper about radioactive waste. Because you have a defined topic, you can go immediately to one of the keyword search engines such as Google, http://www.google.com. Connecting to Google, you receive a screen that allows you to type in keywords such as *radioactive waste.*

Typing two keywords such as *radioactive* and *waste*, however, is asking the search engine to look for sites that have either word, not both words. In this case, the search engine will return an unmanageable number of hits. You can narrow your search by using quote marks around the words "radioactive waste," which tells the search engine that the two words should appear together in that order.

Google, however, provides you a customized form to narrow your search. Click on *Advanced Search* and you will see this screen, which allows you to indicate whether certain topics are relevant to your search or not.

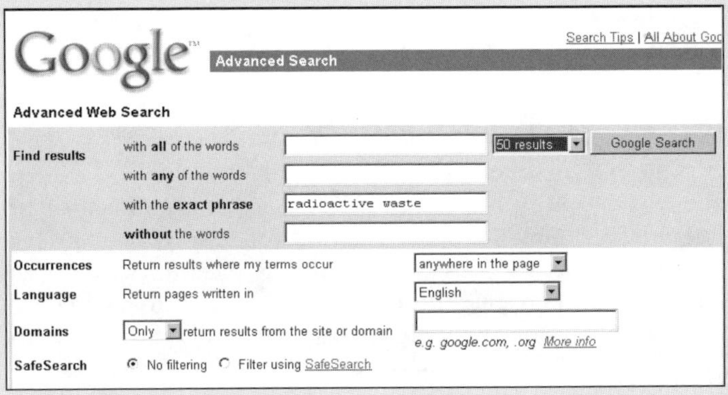

SELECTED META SEARCH ENGINES

Even the best general search engines only access part of the Web. You can solve this problem by using one of the meta search engines which access several search engines.

C4
http://www.C4.com
Searches up to 16 search engines and presents results in groups of ten, with duplicates included.

InfoZoid
http://www.infozoid.com
Searches eight search engines and offers the option to control searches and description for listings. Results include redundant entries.

Ixquick
http://www.izquick.com
Searches 14 search engines, and ranks results by relevancy. Identifies which search engine the entry came from. Supports regular searches, natural language searches, and advanced boolean searches.

RedeSearch
http://www.redesearch.com
Searches ten popular search engines. Organizes listing by search engine which results in redundant listings.

Search Engine Review Sites

If you want to become an expert at finding the most efficient search engines and utilizing them in the most effective ways, check out one of the search engine review sites such as Search Engine Watch, (www.searchenginewatch.com), SearchIQ, (http://www.searchiq.com) or Search Engine Showdown (www.notess.com/search).

MAGAZINES AND NEWSPAPERS

Fortune, the *New York Times*, *Time*, *Wired* magazine—numerous print publications are moving onto the Web, offering full-text articles in special editions or complete Web versions of the print publications. Many also offer search features for the current edition and sometimes for back issues.

Like other resources on the Web, several avenues exist to reach these publications, but no one functional and polished interface accesses all publications you might want to consult. If you know the name of the publication, try locating it directly through one of the keyword search engines.

For magazines and newspapers also try Newsdirectory, http://www.newsdirectory.com. For magazines, look at MagazinesAtoZ.com, http://www.magazinesatoz.com; Magazine Rack, http://www.magazine-rack.com; Yahoo!'s magazine list, http://dir.yahoo.com/News_and_Media/Magazines, which is organized by category, or one of the other search engine's lists of magazines.

For newspapers, try Internet Public Library, http://www.ipl.org/reading/news; OnlineNewspapers.com, http://www.onlinenewspapers.com; Newspapers.com, http://www.newspapers.com; Yahoo!'s list, http://dir.yahoo.com/News_and_Media/Newspapers; or another search engine's list. For U.S. newspapers, try About at http://usnewspapers.about.com/newsissues/usenewspapers

Sample Search

Magazines and Newspapers

Browsing on the Web through a prominent magazine such as *Time* or *Newsweek* may give you ideas for a term paper topic. Or you may already have a topic, and you may want to get a sense of what is going on currently in that subject area. You can connect to *Time* at http://www.time.com and *Newsweek* at http://www.newsweek.com.

If you were looking at the issue of *Newsweek* pictured below, for example, you would see that the Oscars are a hot topic, and it may give you ideas for a term paper about the politics behind the Oscars. You have one article and an idea, so you can now research the Web for more research materials.

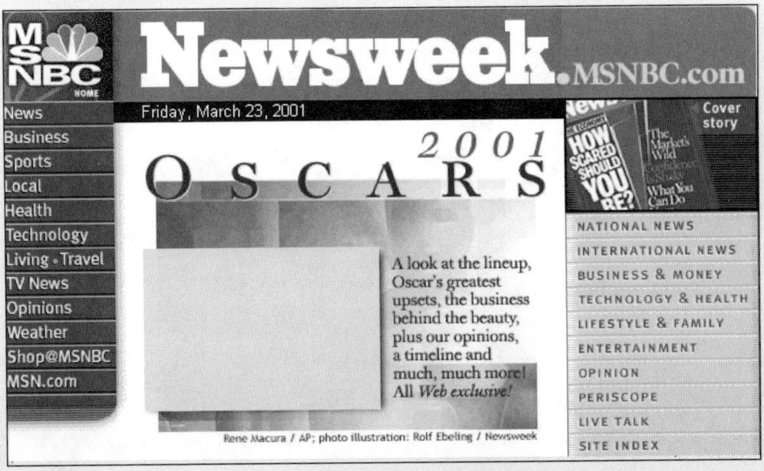

Glancing through Newsweek magazines, you might find a topic that interests you.

EXAMPLES OF POPULAR MAGAZINES AND NEWSPAPERS WITH ONLINE EDITIONS

Business Week	http://www.businessweek.com
New York Times	http://www.nytimes.com
Smithsonian Magazine	http://www.smithsonianmag.si.edu
Time	http://www.time.com
USA Today	http://www.usatoday.com
U.S. News Online	http://www.usnews.com/usnews/home.htm
Wired	http://www.wired.com/wired/current.html

LIBRARIES' FULL-TEXT DATABASES

Most college and university libraries offer CD-Rom magazine and newspaper full-text databases on computers in their libraries. Often these same databases are accessible through a library's Web page, though access may be restricted to students and faculty. ProQuest Direct, Periodical Abstracts (via Ovid), FirstSearch, Infotrac, and EBSCOhost are good examples of general databases. More specialized databases are also available in many fields Often, databases index 2000 to 3000 journals, magazines, and/or newspapers; and they are searchable by title, author, and key word. The databases provide bibliographic information, abstracts, and, in many cases, full-text articles.

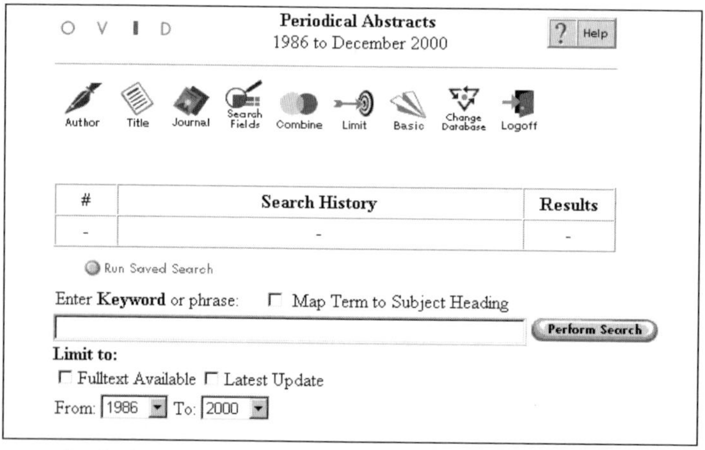

Periodical Abstracts (via Ovid) is one of several full-text databases offering magazine, journal, and newspaper articles through university libraries and their Websites.

Used with permission of Ovid Technologies, Inc.

Librarians' Subject Indexes

One of the best ways to learn about Internet resources is through several indexing projects major libraries sponsor. Librarians have personally reviewed and selected Websites that are of value to academic researchers, including both students and faculty. These indexing Websites are organized by subject area, though most also have keyword search engines as well. You might find it useful to bypass traditional search engines such as Lycos and Excite and to begin research for a term paper with these subject indexes. Thus, you might quickly locate the most authoritative Websites without having to wade through masses of sites looking for the reliable ones. All of these indexes are organized somewhat differently, so you might want to browse through them and select two or three that look user friendly to you.

BUBL LINK

http://bubl.ac.uk/link

BUBL LINK uses the librarian's Dewey Decimal Classification (DDC) to build an Internet subject-oriented resource list. Links are chosen by librarians for their usefulness to academic researchers. The list catalogues over 11,000 resources, a small number compared to search engines, but these are carefully selected resources in all academic disciplines.

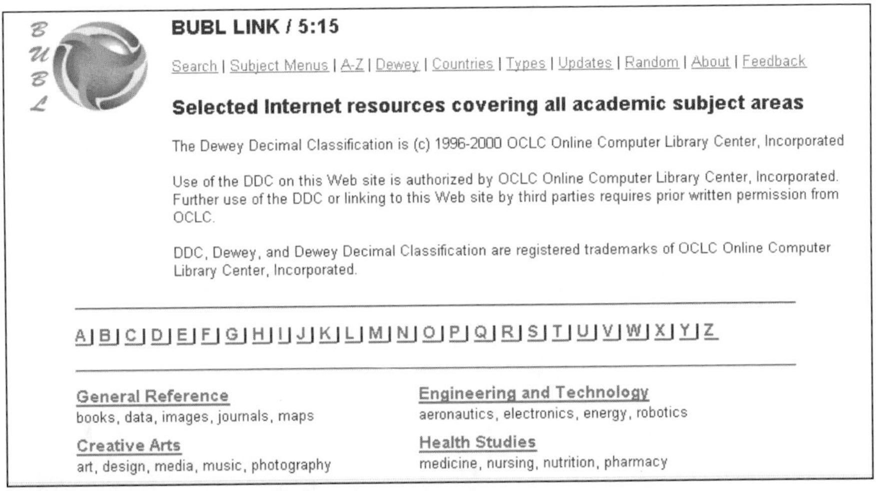

Used with permission. © 2001 BUBL

INFOMINE

http://lib-www.ucr.edu

Sponsored by the University of California at Riverside, Infomine offers links to research resources of interest to students and faculty. It is divided into major collections: biological, agricultural, and medical; government information resources; social sciences and humanities (including general reference, business, and library/information studies); physical sciences, engineering, computer science, and mathematics; Internet enabling tools; maps and geographic information systems; visual and performing arts; and instructional resources of the Internet.

INTERNET PUBLIC LIBRARY

http://www.ipl.org

The Reference Center at the Internet Public Library divides Web resources into sections for arts and humanities, sciences and technology, health and medical sciences, law, government and political science, computers and Internet, business and economics, social sciences, and entertainment and leisure. The "Ask a Question" section allows the user to send a query via MOO form or e-mail, and a real librarian will respond to questions with a factual answer or list of resources within 3–7 days. Lists and links to online books and magazines can be found in the Reading Room. The IPL is designed for K-12 students but is also useful for college students.

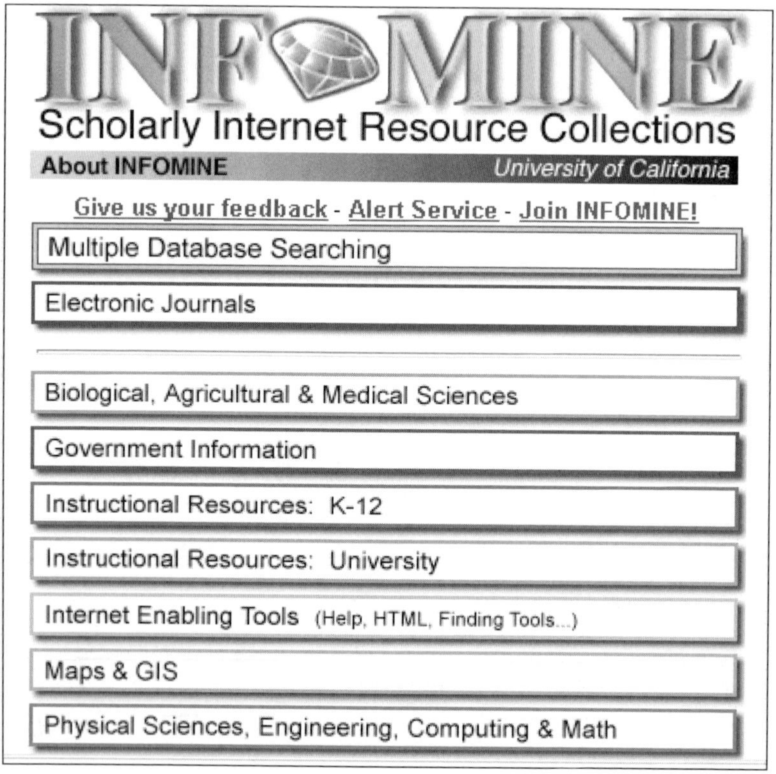

Reprinted by permission with the Regents of the University of California.

INTERNET SCOUT PROJECT

http://scout.cs.wisc.edu/scout/index.html

The Internet Scout Project isn't exactly a library project, but numerous librarians and educators are involved in its indexing. Sponsored by the National Science Foundation, the Internet Scout Project offers timely information to the education community about valuable Internet resources. Among its services is the *Scout Report*, a weekly guide to new Internet resources read by some one hundred thousand people. It can be received either by e-mail or read in the Internet Scout Web pages.

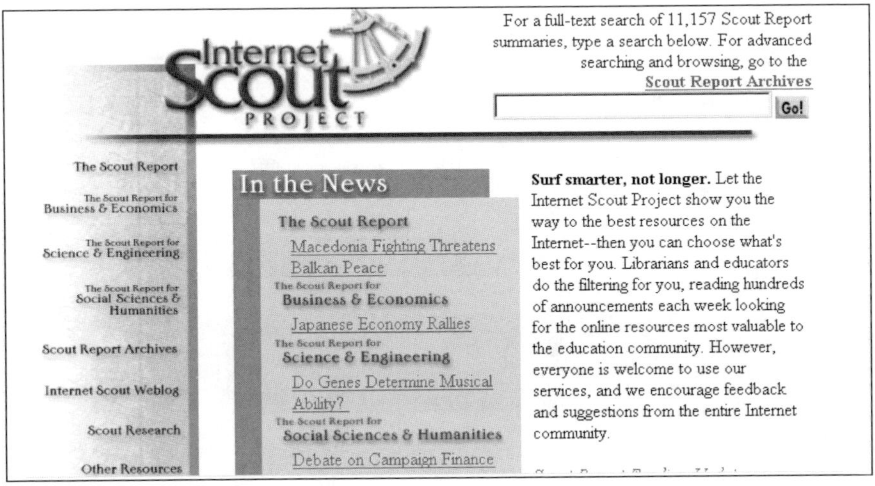

LIBRARIANS' INDEX TO THE INTERNET

http://lii.org/

A searchable subject index, this site lists more than 5000 Internet resources selected and evaluated by librarians at the California State Library. The subject index is arranged in about forty broad categories with subcategories, and the keyword search index has search tips for customized searches. This site is meant to be used by both librarians and non-librarians as a reliable and efficient guide to described and evaluated Internet resources. Supported in part by Federal Library Services and Technology Act finding, it is administered by the California State Library.

MARTINDALES: THE REFERENCE DESK

http://www-sci.lib.uci.edu/~martindale/Ref.html

Located in Australia, Martindales provides an index to online references, including links to thousands of teaching files, multimedia tutorials, and databases in a wide variety of subjects.

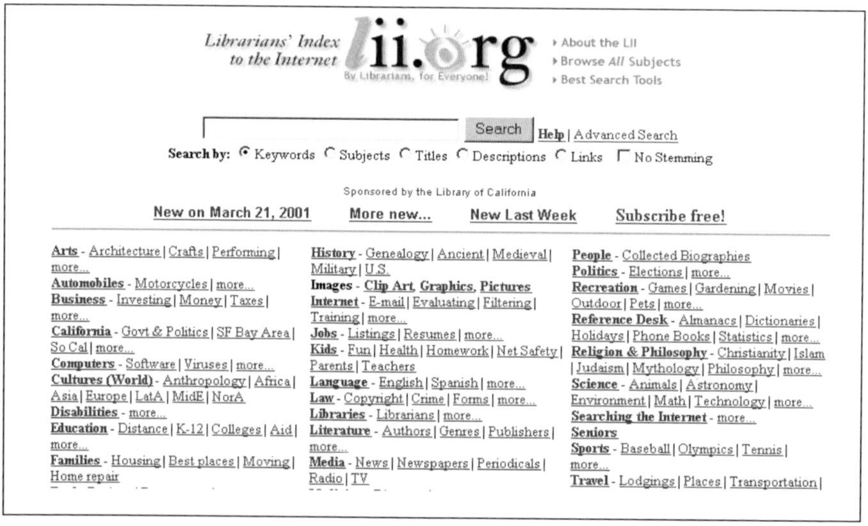

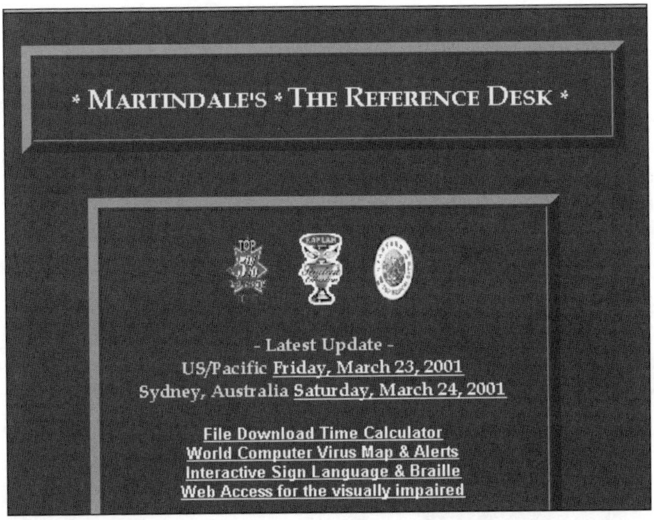

Reprinted with permission from Martindale-Hubbell, a Division of Reed-Elsevier, Inc.

WWW VIRTUAL LIBRARY

http://vlib.org

The WWW Virtual Library is sponsored by CERN, the center for high-energy physics research where the Web was begun. The library is quite extensive, and not all pages are located at CERN. Rather, they are from a collaborative volunteer effort to gather information on a wide variety of topics. The Virtual Library does not offer a keyword search option, but its subject indexes are easy to follow.

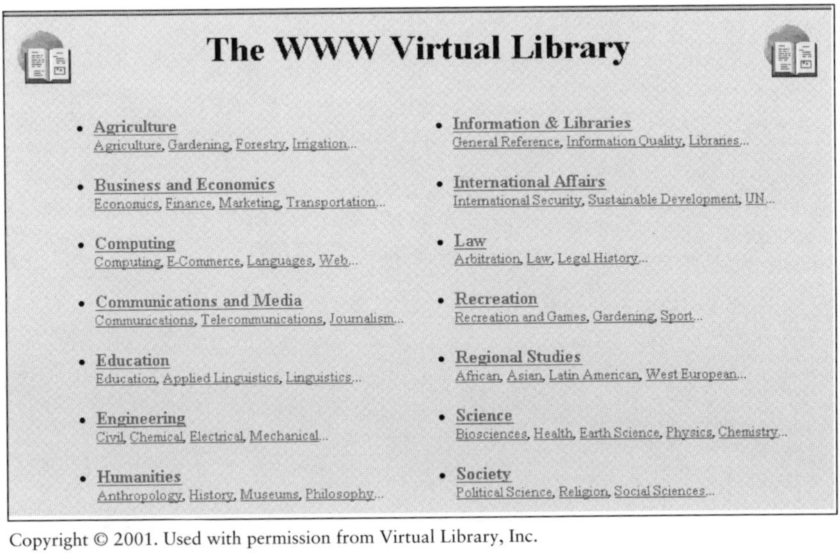

Copyright © 2001. Used with permission from Virtual Library, Inc.

THINGS TO REMEMBER

1. The Web is a fluid medium. What you find today may be gone tomorrow. If you find a useful source, document it thoroughly and keep copies of all of the relevant text portions.
2. If a URL you have doesn't work, do not immediately give up. First, check the address. Web addresses require total accuracy and are uppercase/lowercase sensitive. Often, the pages you are seeking are still on the same computer but have been given a slightly different name. Take the address and cut off the last part. See if that truncated address connects. If it does, look around at the page you find and see if your destination is listed. If this address still does not work, cut off another section and try again.
3. If you are using a search engine, read the directions on the help screens. They will tell you how to customize your search, and this varies widely from one engine to another.
4. Evaluate all material for bias and accuracy. It is very easy to publish on the World Wide Web, and the accuracy of materials varies widely.
5. Be sure to give credit where credit is due. If you find a particular site useful, be sure to reference it in your works cited or reference list.

CHAPTER 4

Email, Email Discussion Groups, and Newsgroups

Email is the most common use of the Internet, exceeding even exploration of the World Wide Web. As a student, you already may use email to communicate with friends and family across the world or across town. If you haven't been initiated yet into the pleasures of this casual and easy communication form, this chapter will provide you with the basics and some examples of email programs.

Increasingly, email is becoming part of the college classroom. Your instructor may have you submit assignments by email or may suggest that you use it as an alternative way to communicate with him or her. You may find it easier to ask your instructor questions by email than you do in class or in an office visit. You also may have a class email discussion group (sometimes informally called a Listserv) or a class mailing list that you use as a forum for discussion of topics related to your classroom studies.

This chapter discusses and demonstrates the basics of email, email discussion groups, and newsgroups. Email discussion groups are mailing lists that you subscribe to, and you receive messages in your email box from members. A discussion of newsgroups (also called Usenet newsgroups), though not accessed by email, is included in this chapter because it provides communication possibilities similar to email discussion groups. You do not subscribe to newsgroups; rather, you access them through a news reader such as the ones included in Internet Explorer and Netscape Communicator.

In addition to class email discussion groups or newsgroups, you can use public groups as additional avenues for research. This chapter will suggest how to find groups discussing topics relevant to your class research. These groups may include other students or professionals in related fields. When you locate a group that seems relevant, it is a good idea to observe the group discussion for several days before you participate. This is called "lurking." After a few days of reading other people's postings, you will have a good idea of how to participate in the discussion. You may ask, for example, for suggestions about Websites, magazine articles, or books that are particularly relevant to your topic. Or you may find that the group offers opinions you can quote in your research paper. Be aware, however, that information posted in email discussion groups and newsgroups generally is opinion, not verifiable fact.

ANATOMY OF AN EMAIL

An email address looks something like this:

login@serveraddress

An example might be john@unm.edu if John is a student at the University of New Mexico. Or, if John has his email account on a commercial server, his address could look like this:

johnj@instantnet.com.

Thus, all email addresses consist of two parts, the individual's log-in name and the server address. The server address may end in .edu if the email account is on a university-owned server. Commercial servers generally have .com or .net endings to their addresses.

When you obtain your email address, you likely will have some choice about a log-in name. Often the log-in name is some version of the person's real name, though sometimes an arbitrary login is assigned. Some individuals prefer to invent a colorful persona for themselves by creating a unique login name. Choose a login that will be easy to remember, both for your memory's sake and for friends who may want to send you mail. Your login name also may be required to log in to your university's email server, and you probably will be asked to declare a password to protect your account.

EMAIL PROGRAMS

Through many university systems, you can access your email through your Web browser. The following brief discussion tells how to use email programs offered by Internet Explorer, as well as Websites that offer free email hosting. Also included is a brief discussion of Pine, an older email program some universities use. If you do not have access to one of these three programs, however, your email program will function in a similar fashion.

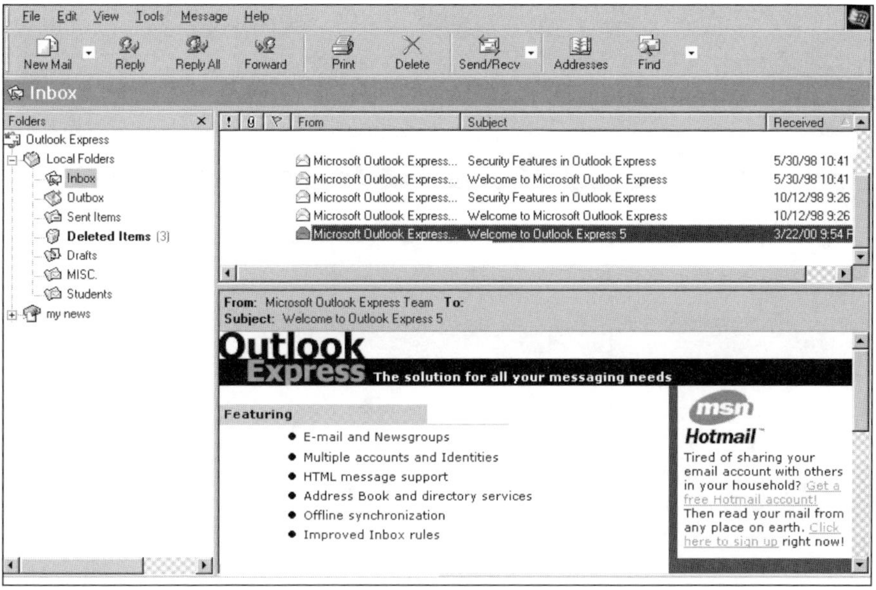

Outlet Express gives you an easy way to send and receive email without leaving the browser.

Internet Explorer Outlook Express

Using Outlook Express with Internet Explorer, you can read your email without leaving the browser. If you want to read your mail, click on the *Mail* icon on the Explorer screen, and choose *Read Mail.* You will see a screen similar to this one:

Your email message will be listed in the upper-right box. You may need to click on *Send and Receive* to download current messages. If you do not have an email or server address indicated in the browser preferences, you may need to specify one, so the browser knows where to locate your email. If you are not prompted by the program to do so, go to the *Tools* menu and select *Accounts.*

Highlight one of your messages by clicking on it, and it will be displayed in the lower right box. After you read the message, you can delete it by clicking *Delete.* You can also save the message in one of your folders listed in the box on the left of the screen. Select the *Edit* menu and choose *Move to Folder.*

If you want to create a message, click on *Compose Message* (or select it from the Explorer main screen by clicking on *New Mail.* The template provides you with spaces for the recipient's email address, any addresses for duplicate copies, a subject line, and attachments. Compose your message in the large box in the lower portion of the screen. When you have finished, you can check your spelling by going to the *Tools* menu. Send your message by clicking *Send.*

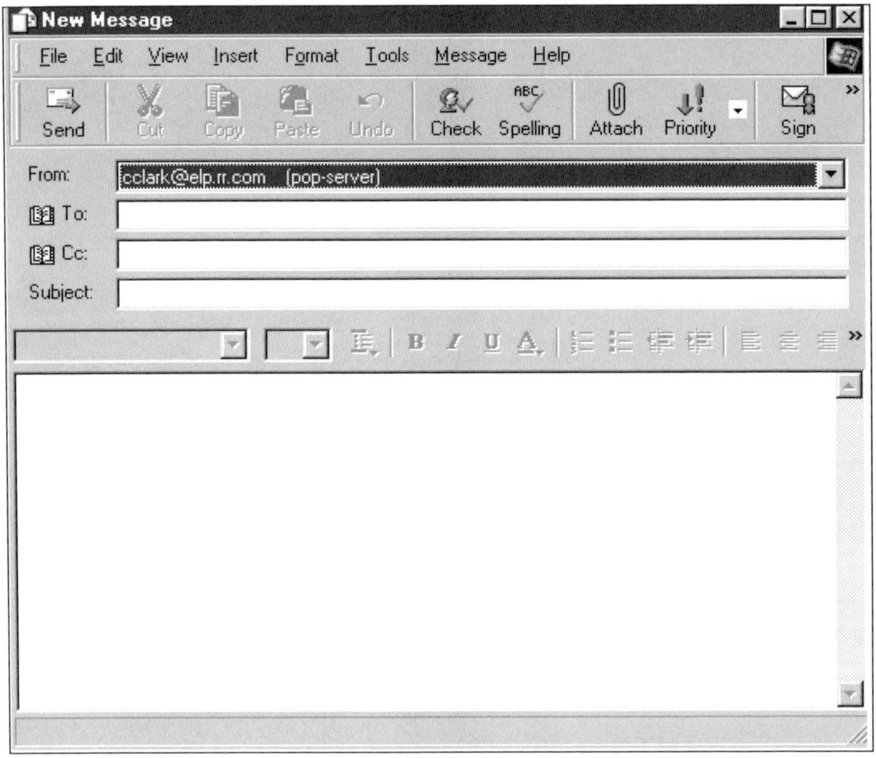

To create a new message in Outlet Express, follow the directions in the template in the top part of the screen and compose your message in the bottom portion.

Outlook Express has many more features you can use to enhance your email communication. Learn about them by exploring the information available through the *Help* menu.

Free Email Hosting Sites

Many Websites offer free email hosting as a way of attracting users to their pages. The appearance and commands of these email programs will vary somewhat, but all will let you read your incoming mail and offer a template for composing and sending new email messages. Generally, you have to register with the site and disclose some demographical information such as income and age which the site can use for marketing.

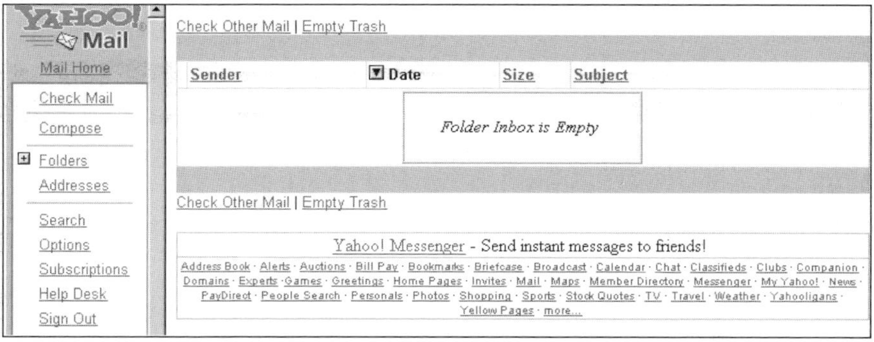

Yahoo is one example of a Website which offers free email hosting.

Pine

An older but efficient email program, Pine is used by many colleges and community organizations that offer text-only access to the Internet. Typically, you access Pine through a menu option when you dial your university's Internet number, or you may Telnet to it (information Telnet allows you to log in to a remote computer network and use its programs). Ask your lab assistant or instructor how to connect to Pine if that is the program available. You will be asked for your log-on information (email address) and a password. Then you will see a welcome screen something like this:

```
?    HELP               -  Get help using Pine

C    COMPOSE MESSAGE    -  Compose and send a message

I    FOLDER INDEX       -  View messages in current folder

L    FOLDER LIST        -  Select a folder to view

A    ADDRESS BOOK       -  Update address book

S    SETUP              -  Configure or update Pine

Q    QUIT               -  Exit the Pine program
```

Pine offers an email option for text-only access to the Internet.

Pine is a menu-driven program with clearly displayed commands and shortcut keys. To compose a message, for example, use your arrow keys to highlight *Compose Message* and press *Enter*. You will see a screen where you can write your email message.

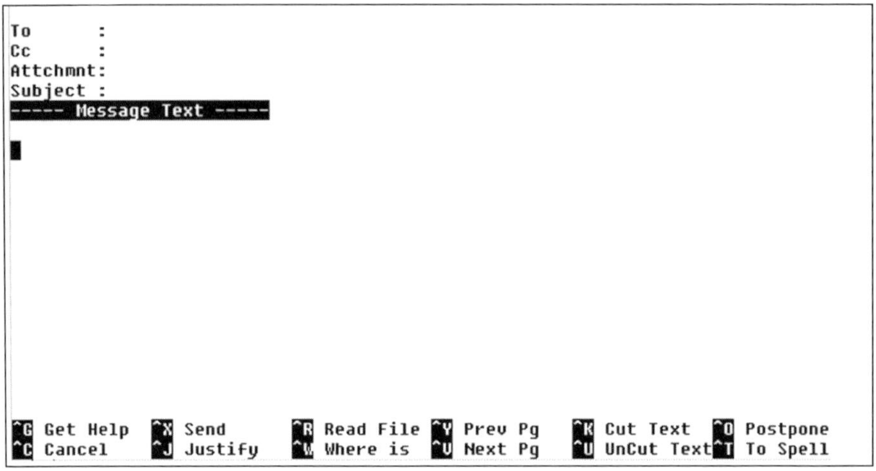

Pine provides a memo-format template for composing an email message.
Reprinted with permission from Martindale-Hubbell, a Division of Reed-Elsevier, Inc.

Notice the list of commands across the bottom of the screen. You can use them to print, spell check, and so forth. To save, for example, press *Control-S.*

To read your mail, select *Folder List* from the opening menu, and press *Enter*. You will see a folder called *Inbox*. Highlight it, and press *Enter* again. You will see a list of your email messages if you have received any. Highlight the email message you want to read, press *Enter*, and you will see the message displayed.

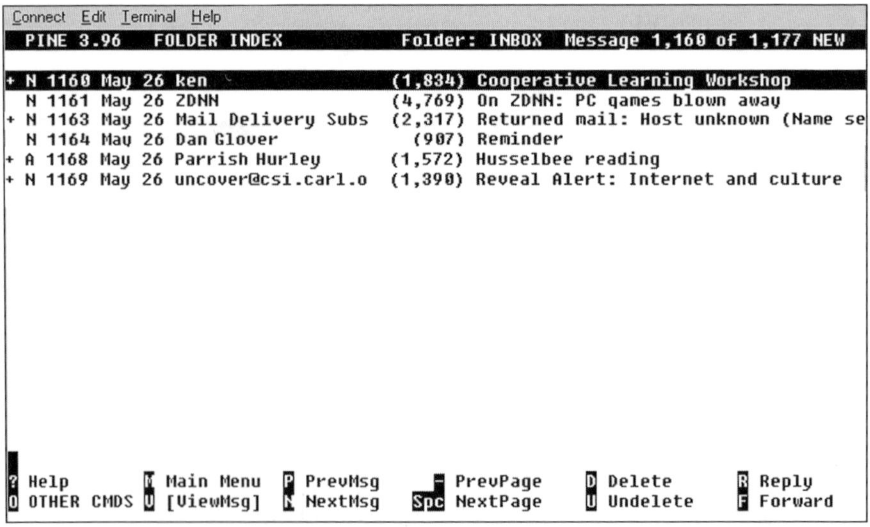

In Pine, the list of email messages look something like this.
Copyright © 2001. Used with permission from Virtual Library, Inc.

Group Discussion via Email and Usenet Newsgroups

Thousands of people communicate every day with others of like interests through two types of discussion groups on the Internet: email discussion groups and newsgroups. The general format of both types is the same. One person sends a message (you can also call it a *posting*) about a topic, which you can identify by the message's subject line. Other people respond about that topic, using the same or similar subject lines and giving their own viewpoint or information. This generates a discussion *thread* or group of posting about the same topic. Threads may last days, weeks, or years, and one discussion group may have numerous threads going at the same time.

You subscribe to email discussion groups, and the postings come to your mailbox. You access newsgroups differently, by connecting to a part of your server that stores the postings of newsgroups. Newsgroups (which may not have anything to do with news or current events) are also called Usenet newsgroups. Both types of discussion groups predate the World Wide Web, though you can access them now through the Web with either Netscape or Explorer. You also can access both types in other ways. Any email program will serve just as well for email discussion groups, and other newsgroup readers are available that do not access newsgroups through the Web.

Email Discussion Groups

(Also Called Listservs or Mailing Lists)

Whether you are interested in discussing current events, accounting for small businesses, or freedom of speech, an email discussion group (sometimes called Listservs or mailing lists) probably exists that matches your interests. Some groups require members to meet certain criteria, such as membership in a college class or having a certain type of degree, but the majority of groups are open to the public. You subscribe to an email discussion group by sending a message to an address managed by an automated program (usually Listserv, Majordomo, or Listproc). Generally, the program subscribes you to the list, sends you a welcome message, and then you begin receiving the group's discussion in the form of email messages members post.

Subscribe and Unsubscribe Commands

Commands such as *subscribe* or *unsubscribe* are sent directly to the list server. Usually that address looks something like this:

listserv@domainname

Listserv-type programs are generally case insensitive, which means you can type *Listserv* or *listserv* and the program will respond to either. If the Listserv address is listserv@xuniversity.edu, you would put that address on the *To*: line of your email message. Other programs utilize addresses similar to majordomo@xcompany.com or listname-request@xcompany.com. Use whatever address you have been given for the group. Leave the subject line blank.

In the message body, you will need to give a subscribe command. These vary slightly depending on which program the server is running, but generally they follow this format:

> Subscribe command: subscribe [listname] [firstname lastname]
> Unsubscribe command: unsubscribe [listname]

For example, if you were subscribing to a Listproc discussion group called apple-1, your message might read:

ubscribe apple-1 James Moffit

After the automated program receives your request for subscription, you will receive a message informing you of commands to use and other information the group wishes subscribers to have. It is a good idea to save this message, for you may want to refer to it later.

Posting Messages to a Group

To post, you send your message to an entirely different address than the one you used to subscribe. Usually the address looks like this:

listname@domainname

You will find the posting address among the directions in your welcome message from the group. Do include a subject line, for many participants may decide whether or not to read a message from what the subject line indicates about the message.

Finding Interesting Groups

Several Websites now offer searchable lists of email discussion groups. Connect to one of these sites, and follow the directions for using its search features to find groups in your area of interest:

CataList

http://www.lsoft.com/lists/listref.html

Liszt

http://www.liszt.com

Directory of Scholarly E-Conferences
http://www.n2h2.com/KOVACS
Publicly Accessible Mailing Lists
http://paml.net

You also can do an email keyword search for a group focusing on a particular topic. Send a message to listserv@listserv.net (or another Listserv maintaining a list of Listservs) including the keywords. The message would look like this:

list global [keywords]

If, for example, you were interested in a group discussing campus conditions, you might use the message list global campus. You would receive a list of email discussion groups with that keyword, and the list would look something like this:

```
ACAA          ACAA@LISTSERV.UIC.EDU
         The Association of Campus Activities Administrators

ACPBEXEC      ACPBEXEC@LISTSERV.KENT.EDU
         Email the executive board of the All Campus Programming Board

ADS           ADS@UPE.AC.ZA
         Adverts on campus

ADVISING-L    ADVISING-L@LISTS.SUNYSB.EDU
         Professional advisors in all divisions of campus.

AGAPEHOUSE    AGAPEHOUSE@LISTSERV.UIC.EDU
         United Campus Ministry at UIC

AGGIEUCM      AGGIEUCM@LISTSERV.TAMU.EDU
         United Campus Ministries in Aggieland

AM-OCAEXEC    AM-OCAEXEC@LISTSERV.TAMU.EDU
         Off Campus Aggies Exec Staff

ANNOUNCE      ANNOUNCE@UMR.EDU
         UMR Campus Computing Services Announcements

AUTHENTICATION-L AUTHENTICATION-L@LISTSERV.UCLA.EDU
         UCLA campus authentication discussion
```

This group list of Email discussion groups having to do with "campus" was obtained from listserv@listserv.net.

NEWSGROUPS

Though the function of newsgroups (sometimes called Usenet newsgroups) is similar in many ways to email discussion groups, they vary in how you access them. As noted earlier, you subscribe to email discussion groups, and the messages come to your mailbox. Newsgroup messages, in contrast, are collected at a central location. You connect to a particular group your Internet provider has subscribed to and read selected messages. An advantage of newsgroups is that the messages are never downloaded to your email, so they do not clog your in-box. On the other hand, you have to develop the habit of checking your group messages, or you do not get the benefits of participating in a group discussion.

Newsgroups are broken into categories that are indicated by a prefix to the name of the group. The most common prefixes are

alt	alternative—broad range of topics
biz	business
comp	computers, computer science
misc	other
news	news about newsgroups
rec	recreation and hobbies
sci	scientific
soc	social issues
talk	debate

The prefix is followed by one or more specific subject names. For example, news.newusers.questions is a group that answers questions from new participants in newsgroups.

Reading Newsgroups in Internet Explorer

To access newsgroups in Internet Explorer, go the *Mail* menu and select *Read News*. If you are using Microsoft Outlook Express as your newsgroup reader, your screen will appear like the one here.

In the box on the left side you will find listed the newsgroups you are subscribed to. If you click on the name of one of the groups, it will display a list of unread messages in the top right box. Click on a message, and it will appear in the lower right box. In this example, the group *news.announce.newusers* is highlighted, a group where announcements are posted about newsgroups. Select a message, and it will appear in the lower box on the right.

If you have no groups listed in the box on the right of the screen or if you want to subscribe to additional groups, click on *News groups*. You will receive this box, where you can review newsgroups your provider has subscribed to:

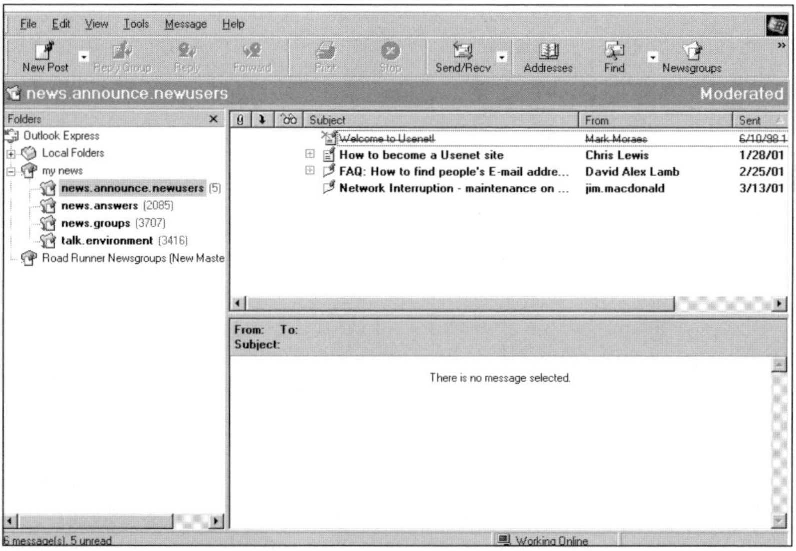

Internet Explorer provides a built-in news reader.

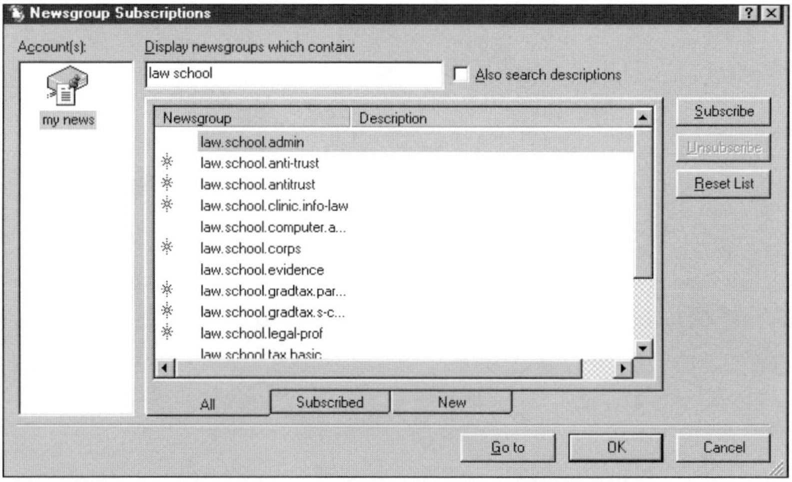

Outlet Express allows you to search newsgroups by key word.

You can type in a keyword in the box, and Outlook Express will list the groups that include that keyword in the name of their group. In the screen illustrated, the words *law school* were entered, and groups are listed that include that word. You can then decide to subscribe to one or more groups.

When you have a group selected and you want to post a message to it, click on *New Post*. If you want to reply to a posted message, click on *Reply Group*. If you want to send a message only to the author of the message you have been reading, click on *Reply*. In each case, you will receive a box where you can type your message; then click on *Send*, which you will find in the *File* menu.

Finding Relevant Groups

As described previously, news-reading software such as Internet Explorer have a keyword search function that can be used to find groups, but this will not work for groups that use abbreviations for their names. Try a keyword search at one of the sources for group archives and information, such as Google (formerly DejaNews archive) at http://www.google.com, Liszt's Usenet Newsgroups Directory at http://www.liszt.com/news, Usenet Info Center Launch Pad at http://www.ibiblio.org/usenet-i, or Cyberfiber, http://www.cyberfiber.com. You can locate the name of a group in the archives and then access newsgroups through your browser and read what is going on currently with the same group.

CHAPTER 5

DOCUMENTING INTERNET SOURCES

To use the extensive resource materials available on the World Wide Web in research projects, you must document your sources. This allows your audience, should they be interested, to retrace your research steps and look at the materials you have used. To do this, you need to provide references in the text to the materials you have used and at the end of your paper furnish a works-cited or reference page. Be aware, however, that Web addresses change and sources sometimes disappear. It is advisable to print out or save on disk any reference material crucial to your research. You can, thus, continually refer to the material, and you can, if necessary, provide a copy for your instructor.

Because the use of Internet sources has grown so quickly, conventions for documenting Web sources are still developing. Check with your professor first about his or her preferences for documenting online sources. You may find handbooks or sites on the Web that suggest somewhat different approaches to documentation of Web sources. This chapter offers models for citing sources that are consistent with Modern Language Association (MLA) and American Psychological Association (APA) styles.

MODERN LANGUAGE ASSOCIATION STYLE

For MLA style, also refer to the *MLA Handbook for Writers of Research Papers* and the MLA Website, http://www.mla.org.

In-Text Citation

Modern Language Association style uses parenthetical (in-text) references that are keyed to a works-cited page at the end of the paper. For print sources, the name of the author and the page number provide the references. This type of citation is difficult for Web sources because few have page numbers, and many do not have specified authors. If you have an author and page or section number, give them. If no author is specified, use a shortened part of the title of the text.

EXAMPLE

According to an *Internet World* article, "Job Trak, the nation's leading online job listing service, claims to have already been used by more than a million students and alumni, with more than 150,000 employers and 300 college career centers posting new jobs daily" (Grusky).

Works-Cited Page

Ideally, a works-cited page provides sufficient information about all the sources you have used so that your readers can locate the materials should they wish to do so. For Web sources, pages change or disappear; thus, you need to include the date you accessed the site in addition to any publication date the source specified.

These are some examples of typical documents you might need to reference:

1. **Book:**

   Give both the date of publication and the date of access.

   Reilly, Bernard F., Jr., *Library of Congress Prints and Photographs: An Illustrated Guide with a Preface by Stephen E. Ostrow*. Washington: Library of Congress, 1995. Library of Congress. 24 March 2001 <http://www.loc.gov/rr/print/guide>.

2. **An article in a magazine:**

   Give both the date of publication and the date of access.

   Baird, Sara. "Mom's a Head-Banger." *Salon*. 7 Oct. 1977. 20 March 2001 <http://www.salonmagazine.com/mwt/feature/1997/10/07rock.html>

3. **A journal article:**

   Kraut, Robert, & Lundmark, Vicki (1998). "Internet Paradox: A Social Technology That Reduces Social Involvement and Psychological Well-Being?" *American Psychologist* 53 (1998): 22 March 2001 <http://www.apa.org/journals/amp/amp5391017.html>

4. **Professional Website:**

   Virtual Computer Library. U of Texas. 22 March 2001 <http://www.utexas.edu/computer/vcl>

5. **Commercial Website page:**

   Vacation and Last-minute Specials. American Express. 24 March 2001 <http://travel.americanexpress.com/travel/lmt/default.asp?bcid=1&lmt=1_home=travlastmin>

6. **Personal Website:**

   Barlow, John Perry. Home page. 22 March 2001 <http://www.eff.org/%7Ebarlow/barlow.html>.

7. **Scholarly project:**

   Rhetoric and Composition. 29 Nov. 1996. University of Washington. 24 March 2001. <http://eserver.org/rhetoric>

8. **Article in a subscription database:**

   Linn, Susan. "Sellouts." *American Prospect*. 23 Oct. 2000: 17-20. *Periodical Abstracts*. University of Texas at El Paso Library, El Paso, TX. 15 March 2001 <http://libraryweb.utep.edu/eriodicalabatracts>

American Psychological Association Style

For APA style, also refer to the *Publication Manual of the American Psychological Association* and the APA Website, http://www.apastyle.org

In-Text Citations

American Psychological Association style specifies giving the author and date after referenced material in the text and giving author, date, and page numbers after quotations. This type of citation is difficult for Web sources because many texts do not have specified authors or dates of publication. If you have an author and date of publication, give them. If no author is specified, use a shortened part of the title of the text.

EXAMPLE

According to an *Internet World* article, "Job Trak, the nation's leading online job listing service, claims to have already been used by more than a million students and alumni, with more than 150,000 employers and 300 college career centers posting new jobs daily" (Grusky, 1996).

The APA also suggests citing Website home pages by giving the address in the text (e.g., http://www.apa.org). No citation on the reference page is needed. For specific articles posted on the World Wide Web, always cite the article in the reference list and include "retrieved from" and the date.

Reference List

Instead of a works-cited page, APA specifies a reference list. Since you can cite Web page addresses in the text, according to the APA Web page, you would put Web references in the reference list only if they refer to specific articles or books published on the World Wide Web.

EXAMPLES

Kraut, R., & Lundmark, V. (1998). Internet paradox: A social technology that reduces social involvement and psychological well-being? *American Psychologist,* 53, pp. 1017-1031. Retrieved April 15, 2000, from the World Wide Web: http://www.apa.org/journals/amp/amp5391017.html

Electronic reference formats recommended by the American Psychological Association. (2001, January 10). Washington, DC: American Psychological Association. Retrieved March 22, 2001, from the World Wide Web: http://www.apa.org/journals/webref.html

Article in an electronic database

Linn, S. (2000, Oct. 23) Sellouts. *American Prospect,* 11(22), pp. 17-20. Retrieved March 15, 2001, from *Periodical Abstracts* database, accession number 62528011, on the World Wide Web: http://libraryweb.utep.edu/periodicalabatracts

CHAPTER 6

INTERNET ACTIVITIES FOR *PRINCIPLES OF ECONOMICS*, THIRD EDITION BY N. GREGORY MANKIW

CHAPTER 1: TEN PRINCIPLES OF ECONOMICS

1. What Do Economists Do?

   Go to http://www.bls.gov/oco. Search for the occupation "economist." In one paragraph, what does an economist do? About how many economists were employed in the most recent year? What are the training and qualifications to be an economist? What is the job outlook for economists?

2. Where Are We in the Business Cycle?

   Go to http://www.nber.org/cycles.html. What was the date of the most recent business cycle peak? Trough? What phase of the business cycle are we currently in?

3. I, Pencil

   Go to http://209.217.49.168/vnews.php?nid=316. What is the *invisible hand* and how is this story an example of the *invisible hand* at work?

CHAPTER 2: THINKING LIKE AN ECONOMIST

1. The President's Council of Economic Advisers

   Go to http://www.whitehouse.gov/cea. What does the Council of Economic Advisors do? Who are the members of the Council and who is the chair?

2. Realism and Economic Models

   Go to http://www.mapquest.com. Select "Driving Directions" and find a route between your hometown and the college or university you are attending. The directions are accompanied by a map. Study the map. Is the map "realistic?" Could you still use the map to get where you are going? What is the relationship between a map and an economic model? Is realism an essential component of an economic model?

3. Graphing the Poverty Rate

   Go to http://www.census.gov/hhes/www/poverty.html. Find and graph the poverty rate for families during your lifetime. Has the poverty problem improved or gotten worse?

CHAPTER 3: INTERDEPENDENCE AND THE GAINS FROM TRADE

1. TicketMaster and Ticket Prices

   Go to http://www.ticketmaster.com. What would two tickets cost to an event of your choice (remember to include all the relevant service charges)? Be careful not to actually buy the tickets unless you really want to. Is purchasing through Ticketmaster cheaper or more expensive than buying the tickets directly from the box office?

2. Occupational Specialization

   Go to http://www.bls.gov/oes/home.htm#overview. How many people in the United States have specialized as Retail Salespersons, Dentists, Kindergarten Teachers, and Airline Pilots, Copilots and Flight Engineers?

Chapter 4: The Market Forces of Supply and Demand

1. The Price of Gold

   Go to http://www.goldkit.com. What was the market price of gold at the time you accessed the page? Do not forget to mention when you accessed the page. Was the price of gold rising or falling? Draw a graph to show why the price of gold rose or fell.

2. Advertising and Demand

   Go to http://www.msnbc.com. How many advertisements appeared on the page? Using a demand and supply diagram, show what effect the advertiser hopes to have.

Chapter 5: Elasticity and Its Applications

1. Price Elasticity of Demand for a Web Page

   Go to http://www.usatoday.com. How much did you pay to use the page? What do you think would happen to usage of the page if users were charged $.25 each time they accessed the page? Do you think the price elasticity of demand is high or low? Explain using the determinants of price elasticity of demand.

2. OPEC

   Go to http://www.opec.org. What is OPEC? Why does OPEC find it difficult to keep the price of oil high?

CHAPTER 6: SUPPLY, DEMAND, AND GOVERNMENT POLICIES

1. The Minimum Wage

   Go to http://www.dol.gov/esa/minwage/america.htm. What is the minimum wage in your state?

2. Tipped Employees

   Go to http://www.dol.gov/esa/regs/compliance/whd/mwposter.htm. What is a "tipped employee?" What is the minimum wage for a "tipped employee?" What do you think about "tipped employees" having a lower minimum wage than everyone else?

3. The Payroll Tax

   Go to http://www.ssa.gov. What is the current tax rate and earnings limit applicable to employees and employers (it might take some searching of the Web page)? Do you think employees and employers actually share the burden of the tax equally?

CHAPTER 7: CONSUMERS, PRODUCERS, AND THE EFFICIENCY OF MARKETS

1. The eBay Experience

   Go to http://www.ebay.com. Describe how eBay works. Are the outcomes on eBay economically efficient?

2. Dutch Auctions

   Go to http://www.batky-howell.com/~jb/auction. How does a Dutch auction work? How does it differ from the auction used to sell the Elvis Presley album in Chapter 7? Under which type of auction arrangement do you think the buyer fares better?

Chapter 8: Application: The Costs of Taxation

1. Tax Preparation Time

   Go to http://www.irs.gov/forms_pubs/forms.html. Scroll to "Inst 1040 (General Inst) Instructions for Form 1040" (instructions on how to fill out Form 1040—the tax form most Americans use for their income tax). Find the table with "Estimated Preparation Time" for various tax forms (it is toward the back of the booklet). How long does it take the average taxpayer to prepare Form 1040? How would you calculate how much it costs the average taxpayer to fill out the form? Is this cost part of the deadweight loss of taxation? Explain.

2. States Sales Taxes

   Go to http://www.taxadmin.org/fta/rate/sales.html. How many states exempt food and prescription drugs from sales taxation? Write a short essay discussing the exemption of these two items from the standpoints of efficiency and equity.

3. Henry George's Remedy: Is It Right? Will It Work?

   Go to http://www.henrygeorge.org/rem0.htm. Write a short essay discussing Henry George's single tax on land from the standpoints of efficiency and equity.

Chapter 9: Application: International Trade

1. What is the WTO?

   Go to http://www.wto.org/english/thewto_e/whatis_e/whatis_e.htm. Using the information from this World Trade Organization (WTO) sponsored Web page, write a short essay and what the WTO is and does.

2. What is the United States International Trade Commission?

   Go to http://www.usitc.gov/geninfo.htm#ITC_is. What is the United States International Trade Commission and what does it do?

CHAPTER 10: EXTERNALITIES

1. Patents and Trademarks

   Go to http://www.uspto.gov, the United States Patent and Trademark Office Web site. Briefly explain how to obtain either a patent or a trademark (your choice). Using the theory of externalities, explain why the government protects patents and trademarks.

2. Acid Rain

   Go to http://www.epa.gov/oar/oaqps/peg_caa/pegcaa05.html#topic5. What is acid rain? Explain why it is likely to be a source of externality problems.

CHAPTER 11: PUBLIC GOODS AND COMMON RESOURCES

1. The Characteristics of a Web Page

   Go to http://www.epa.gov/oar/oaqps/peg_caa/pegcaa05.html#topic5. What information is available on this page? Is the information excludable? Rival? What type of good is this information?

2. Endangered Species

   Go to http://endangered.fws.gov/wildlife.html#Species. Find an endangered species that interests you. Can the market be relied on to protect this species? Explain.

CHAPTER 12: THE DESIGN OF THE TAX SYSTEM

1. Marginal and Average Tax Rates

   Go to http://www.irs.gov/forms_pubs/forms.html. Scroll to "Inst 1040 (Tax Tables) Tax Table and Tax Rate Schedules" for the most recent year. Find the "Tax Rate Schedules" (near the back). What are the average and marginal tax rates for a single individual with a taxable income of \$20,000, \$40,000, \$80,000, \$160,000, and \$320,000?

2. Federal Spending and Taxation

   Go to http://w3.access.gpo.gov/eop. From the most recent edition of *The Economic Report of the President,* find federal spending and taxes by the categories in Tables 4 and 5 in your textbook.

CHAPTER 13: THE COSTS OF PRODUCTION

1. Marginal and Average Cost

   Use the National Basketball Association's (http://www.nba.com) or Women's National Basketball Association's (http://www.wnba.com) Web site to find your favorite star's season scoring average and how many points he (or she) scored in his/her most recent game. Did his/her scoring in that game raise or lower his/her season scoring average? What is the relevance of this problem to the relationship between marginal cost and average total cost? If basketball is not your game, modify this problem using football (http://www.nfl.com), baseball (http://mlb.mlb.com/NASApp/mlb/mlb/homepage/mlb_homepage.jsp), or hockey (http://www.nhl.com).

2. Operating a Web Site

   Go to http://w3.access.gpo.gov/eop. What is the marginal cost to Best Buy of serving another customer at its Web site?

CHAPTER 14: FIRMS IN COMPETITIVE MARKETS

1. Florida Citrus Web Site

   Go to http://www.floridajuice.com. The "Florida Citrus Web Site" is sponsored by the Florida Department of Citrus on behalf of the State's Orange Industry. Among other things, the site is clearly an advertisement for the state's orange industry. Have you ever seen or do you expect to see advertising for individual orange growers? Why? In terms of demand and supply, what is the purpose of the Florida Citrus Web Site?

2. School Vouchers

   Go to http://www.schoolchoices.org. What do supporters of school vouchers believe vouchers will accomplish? How can the theory of competitive markets discussed in the chapter be used to support the case for school vouchers? Do you think school vouchers are likely to be effective? Why or why not?

CHAPTER 15: MONOPOLY

1. Mergers

   Go to http://www.ftc.gov/bc/compguide. What is a horizontal merger, vertical merger, and potential competition merger? Give a hypothetical example of each. Why are mergers scrutinized by the antitrust authorities?

2. Bottled Water

   Go to http://www.perrier.com. Is this product produced by a monopoly firm? Explain.

CHAPTER 16: OLIGOPOLY

1. The OPEC Oil Cartel

   Go to http://www.opec.org. What are the organization's stated goals, which countries are members, and when was it founded? According to your textbook, OPEC has had trouble keeping prices high. Why was that the case? Can you think of any reasons why the members of OPEC might find it difficult to cooperate with each other?

2. The Federal Trade Commission

   Go to http://www.ftc.gov. What is the FTC and what role does in play in promoting competition?

3. Antitrust Enforcement and the Consumer

   Go to http://www.usdoj.gov/atr/public/div_stats/9142.htm. This is the U.S. Department of Justice's view of its role in antitrust enforcement. According to the Department of Justice, what stake do consumers have in antitrust enforcement?

Chapter 17: Monopolistic Competition

1. Monopolistic Competition on the Web

   Go to http://www.msn.com, http://www.aol.com, and http://www.cs.com. Browse around each page. Are these three internet services participating in a monopolistically competitive market? Explain.

2. Valuable Advertising?

   Go to http://www.washingtonpost.com. How many advertisements are on the page? Do you consider this advertising valuable or wasteful from a social standpoint? Explain.

Chapter 18: The Markets for the Factors of Production

1. National Income and Payments to the Factors of Production

   Go to http://www.bea.gov/bea/dn1.htm. Select the most recent "GDP News Release." Go to Table 8 and find National Income for the most recent year. What are the five main components of National Income? What factor of production earns each type of income? What percentage of the total National Income goes to each of these categories?

2. Labor Supply

   Go to http://www.bls.gov/ces/home.htm#overview. What has happened to total hours of work in the United States in the last month? Is total hours the best measure of labor supply?

Chapter 19: Earnings and Discrimination

1. Family Income and Discrimination

   Go to http://www.census.gov/hhes/www/income.html. Select the report "Money Income in the United States" for the most recent year. Find the median family income for whites, blacks, and Hispanics for the most recent year. Are the differences evidence of labor market discrimination? Explain.

2. Weekly Earnings by Race and Gender

   Go to http://www.bls.gov/cps/home.htm. Find the document "Usual Weekly Earnings of Wage and Salary Workers." Create a bar graph showing median weekly earnings for the most recent quarter by race and gender.

CHAPTER 20: INCOME INEQUALITY AND POVERTY

1. The Lorenz Curve

   Go to http://www.mwc.edu/econ/RycE202/L/l.htm. This site has a computer-based tutorial about the Lorenz curve and an exercise. Complete the exercise and submit it to your instructor.

2. The Poverty Rate

   Go to http://www.census.gov/hhes/www/poverty01.html. Find the number of people who are poor and the poverty rate for the most recent year.

3. Counting the Number of Poor People

   Go to http://www.census.gov/hhes/poverty/poverty01/tables01.html. Find the poverty thresholds for the most recent year for families ranging in size from one to nine or more persons.

4. Ending Poverty

   Go to http://www.census.gov/hhes/poverty/poverty01/tables01.html and find the table "Income Deficit or Surplus of Families and Unrelated Individuals by Poverty Status." How many poor families are there and what is their average income deficit? Will multiplying the number of poor families by their average income deficit give the amount of money needed to eliminate poverty among families in the United States? Explain.

CHAPTER 21: THE THEORY OF CONSUMER CHOICE

1. Your Budget Constraint

   Go to http://www.amazon.com. Find the price of your favorite movie (in DVD format). Find the price of a book that interests you. (In both cases, ignore shipping and handling.) (a) Assume you have $200 to spend and the movie and the book are the only goods available. Graph your budget constraint and explain how you constructed it. (b) Now assume you have $300 to spend. Graph your new budget constraint. (c) Finally, assuming you have $200 to spend, add $5 to the price of the movie and graph your budget constraint.

2. Food Stamps

   Go to http://www.fns.usda.gov/fsp. Find the maximum monthly allotment of food stamps for a family of three, four, and five persons. You will have to do some searching to find the information.

CHAPTER 22: FRONTIERS OF MICROECONOMICS

1. The Rational Voter

   Go to http://www.fec.gov/elections.html. What percentage of the eligible voters actually voted in the most recent presidential election? In how many states was the winner of the presidential electoral votes decided by only one vote? Is there a link between the two outcomes?

2. Free Riding

   Go to http://www.marietta.edu/~delemeeg/games/table1.htm. Find a game dealing with public goods or free riding. Explain how the game works. How would a rational player play the game? What do you think will actually happen?

CHAPTER 23: MEASURING A NATION'S INCOME

1. GDP

   Go to http://www.bea.gov. Find data on Nominal GDP, Real GDP, and the GDP Deflator for the most recent year.

2. Components of GDP

   Go to http://www.bea.gov. Find data on the components of GDP for the most recent year.

3. GDP and Well-being

   Go to http://www.census.gov/statab/www. Do you feel well-being in society has increased or decreased during your lifetime? Why? Find data on real GDP and population in the year of your birth and the most recent year. Compute per capita real GDP both years. Has it increased or decreased? Is what happened to real GDP relevant or irrelevant, consistent or inconsistent with what you think happened to social well-being? Explain.

CHAPTER 24: MEASURING THE COST OF LIVING

1. The Rate of Inflation

   Go to http://www.bls.gov. What is the current rate of inflation in the United States?

2. The Value of the Dollar

   Go to http://www.bls.gov and find the link to the Inflation Calculator (it is in the upper left-hand section of the page). The buying power of $100 in the year of your birth is equivalent to how much today?

3. Comparing the Cost of Living in Different Cities

   Go to http://www.homefair.com/homefair/calc/salcalc.html. Enter your hometown (or some place close to it) and the town where you go to college (or some place close to it). What is the difference in the cost of living between the two towns?

4. COLA and Social Security

   Go to http://www.ssa.gov/cola. Social Security benefits to retired recipients are increased annually by the percentage increase in the cost of living. What was the most recent COLA for Social Security recipients? What is the COLA intended to do?

CHAPTER 25: PRODUCTION AND GROWTH

1. Comparative GDP

   Go to http://www.odci.gov/cia/publications/factbook. Choose any three countries from any three continents and find GDP for each.

2. The Magic of Compound Interest

   Go to http://www.1728.com/compint.htm. How much money would you have to deposit today so that you would have $1,000,000 on the day you retire? Assume your deposit will grow 10 percent per year.

3. Catching Up

   Go to http://www.odci.gov/cia/publications/factbook. Find the per capita GDP of the United States and any other country (follow the economy link for that country). Then go to http://www.1728.com/compint.htm. Letting U.S. per capita GDP be "Total" and the other country's per capita GDP be "Principal," how many years would it take that country to achieve the U.S. level of per capita GDP if the country grew at 2 percent, 3 percent, and 4 percent per year? If the United States grew at the same rate, what would the U.S. per capita GDP be after that many years?

CHAPTER 26: SAVING, INVESTMENT, AND THE FINANCIAL SYSTEM

1. The Dow-Jones Industrial Average

   Go to http://www.nyse.com. What was the Dow-Jones Industrial Average at the time you visited the site? What has happened to the Dow-Jones Industrial Average over the last quarter? (Hint: following DJIA links will get you to the answer quickly.)

2. Company Stock Quotes

   Go to http://www.nasdaq.com. Find the stock symbol and most recent price for the stock of a corporation of your choice. (Hint: Use the "Company Search" button to find the stock symbol.)

CHAPTER 27: THE BASIC TOOLS OF FINANCE

1. Winning the Lottery

   Go to http://www.infospace.com/lycos.lotter/lotto/index.htm. Find the most recent jackpot for the Lotto game (pick six numbers) for any state. Assume you won that jackpot and will receive the payoff in equal increments over the next 20 years. What is the present value of your winnings (assume a discount rate of 10 percent)?

2. Index Funds

   Go to http://www.fool.com/school/13steps/stepfour.htm. What are the advantages of investing in index funds? What are the disadvantages?

3. Pick 3

   Go to http://www.valottery.com. What are the chances of winning the "Pick 3 Exact Order" game? How much can you win? What is the expected return? Is paying $1 to play this game rational?

CHAPTER 28: UNEMPLOYMENT AND ITS NATURAL RATE

1. The Unemployment Rate

   Go to http://www.bls.gov. Find the most recent unemployment rate.

2. Unemployment Rate Differences by Age, Gender, and Race

   Go to http://www.bls.gov/ces/home.htm. Read the most recent "Employment Situation Summary." What is the most recent overall unemployment rate and what are the unemployment rates for adult men, adult women, teenagers, whites, blacks, and Hispanic.

3. The "Right-to-Work"

   Go to http://www.right-to-work.org. Following the "About" link, read "Frequently-asked Questions" and "The Problem." What is the Right-to-Work principle? Do you agree or disagree with it?

4. The AFL-CIO

   Go to http://www.afl-cio.org. What is the AFL-CIO? Is the AFL-CIO a union?

CHAPTER 29: THE MONETARY SYSTEM

1. The FOMC

   Go to http://www.federalreserve.gov/fomc. What is the Federal Open Market Committee? Who are its current members?

2. The Board of Governors

   Go to http://www.federalreserve.gov/bios. Who are the current members of the Board of Governors of the Federal Reserve System? Choose one member and write a short paragraph describing the member's background and experience in the field of economics.

3. The Monetary Aggregates

   Go to http://www.federalreserve.gov/releases/h6. For the most recent week, what is the amount of M1, M2, and M3?

CHAPTER 30: MONEY GROWTH AND INFLATION

1. What Is a Dollar Worth?

   Go to http://www.minneapolisfed.org/Research/data/us/calc/index.cfm. What is a dollar worth?

2. The Real Rate of Interest

   Go to http://www.federalreserve.gov/releases/h15/update. Find the interest rate on one-year Treasury securities. What is the real rate of interest on these securities? This page might help: http://www.bls.gov.

CHAPTER 31: OPEN-ECONOMY MACROECONOMICS: BASIC CONCEPTS

1. Trade Deficits and Surpluses

   Go to http://www.whitehouse.gov/fsbr/international.html. Is the United States currently running a trade deficit or surplus?

2. Exchange Rates

   Go to http://moneycentral.msn.com/investor/market/rates.asp. What is the exchange rate between the dollar and a currency of your choice? How many units of that currency would $1,000.00 buy? (Ignore transaction fees.)

3. The Euro

   Go to http://www.euro.ecb.int. What countries currently use the euro? Why are these countries using a common currency?

CHAPTER 32: A MACROECONOMIC THEORY OF THE OPEN ECONOMY

1. Budget Deficits and the Trade Balance

   Go to http://www.fms.treas.gov/mts/index.html. Read "Monthly Treasury Statement." Is the budget in deficit or surplus? According to the model introduced in the chapter, what should happen to the trade balance? Go to http://www.whitehouse.gov/fsbr/esbr.html. What is the current trade balance?

2. The IMF

   Go to http://www.imf.org. Read a paragraph explaining what the IMF does.

Chapter 33: Aggregate Demand and Aggregate Supply

1. The Business Cycle

   Go to http://www.nber.com. The NBER's Business Cycle Dating Committee is a semi-official body that decides the key dates on the business cycle. According to the committee, what phase of the business cycle is the economy currently in? When was the most recent business cycle peak? trough?

2. The Index of Leading Indicators

   Go to http://www.conference-board.org. What is the Index of Leading Indicators? What is it currently saying about the direction of the economy?

Chapter 34: The Influence of Monetary and Fiscal Policy on Aggregate Demand

1. The Beige Book

   Go to http://www.federalreserve.gov/policy.htm. Read the most recent Beige Book summary for the Federal Reserve district you are located in. On the basis of the summary, should monetary policy be expansionary or contractionary in the future?

2. The FOMC Press Release

   Go to http://www.federalreserve.gov/pressreleases.htm. Follow the "Monetary Policy" link and read the most recent "FOMC statement." What is the FOMC's recipe for monetary policy and do you support it?

3. The European Central Bank

   Go to http://www.ecb.int/index.html. Find the document "The European Central Bank." How is the bank similar to the U.S. Federal Reserve System? How is it different?

CHAPTER 35: THE SHORT-RUN TRADEOFF BETWEEN INFLATION AND UNEMPLOYMENT

1. The Misery Index

   Go to http://www.bls.gov. What is the current misery index? (Hint: Since the inflation rate at the link is a monthly rate, it must be "annualized" to be able to compute a misery index comparable to the one mentioned in the textbook. Multiplying the monthly inflation rate by 12 is an adequate approximation for this purpose.)

2. The Phillips Curve

   Go to http://www.bls.gov. Find the annual rate of inflation and rate of unemployment over the last four years. Does there appear to be a tradeoff between inflation and unemployment?

CHAPTER 36: FIVE DEBATES OVER MACROECONOMIC POLICY

1. Inflation Targeting

   Go to http://www.frbsf.org/econrsrch/wklyltr/wklyltr98/el98-18.html. What is inflation targeting and should the Fed adopt that as an operating strategy?

2. Your Share of the Government Debt?

   Go to http://www.publicdebt.treas.gov/opd/opdpdodt.htm. What is your share of the government's debt? You might need information from the Census Bureau site (http://www.census.gov) to help you answer the question.

3. The Flat Tax

   Go to http://flattax.house.gov/welcome.htm. What is the flat tax? Would a flat tax encourage saving?

4. The Consumption Tax

   Go to http://www.fairtax.org. What is the consumption tax? Would a consumption tax encourage saving?

PART I APPENDIX

Sources of Additional Information

General Internet/Web Guides

The Complete Internet Guide and Web Tutorial
http://www.microsoft.com/insider/internet

Internet 101
http://www2.famvid.com/i101

WebNovice
http://www.webnovice.com

Beginners' Central
http://www.northernwebs.com/bc

Exploring the World-Wide Web
http://www.gactr.uga.edu/exploring/index.html

Virtual Computer Library
http://www.utexas.edu/computer/vcl

World Wide Web FAQ
http://www.boutell.com/faq

The World Wide Web for the Clueless
http://www.mit.edu:8001/people/rei/wwwintro.html

Recommended Internet Search Engines & Finding Tools
http://infomine.ucr.edu/guides/index.html

Internet Search Tool Details
http://sunsite.berkeley.edu/Help/searchdetails.html

WebPlaces Internet Search Guide
http://www.webplaces.com

SEARCH ENGINE GUIDES AND REVIEWS

Search Engine Watch
http://www.searchenginewatch.com

SearchIQ
http://www.searchiq.com

Search Engine Showdown
http://www.notess.com/search

PART II

THOMSONLEARNING.COM

Thomson Learning Economics Website Overview

Thomson Learning Website Navigation

Introduction to Economics Topics

Thomson Learning Economics Website Overview

Thomson Learning Website Navigation

This section will help you learn more about Thomson Learning's Website, acquaint you with what is available, where to find it, and how to make it work for you.

Thomson Learning's home page offers both instructors and students the opportunity to discover more about our parent company, Thomson Learning, as well as the many areas of interest from High School Advanced Placement materials to information regarding International Colleges and Universities.

If you know what you want but are unsure where to find it on the site, use the **Search us** tool provided on the home page. This allows you to type in the topic you are looking for and generates a number of possible links to your area of interest.

- ABOUT US links to a brief history of Thomson Learning.

- CONTACT US provides information on how to provide feedback, review employment opportunities, and submit future proposal ideas.

- SHOP US links you directly to our E-store where you can purchase lab manuals, educational software, study guides, and other material not always found in bookstores.

Another way to navigate the Thomson Learning Website is to use the tabs at the top of the home page. Each tab represents a particular page of services to our customers.

- The **E-service** tab represents Thomson Learning's customer relation services from where to find a subject/book to site concerns, like quizzing issues or technical support.
- The **Instructors** tab provides information and tools where instructors can purchase material for their course and develop course syllabi or quizzes.
- The **Students** tab provides you with quick links to tools and information like study aids, online quizzes, and review material.

On the top of the home page click the **Students** tab for more information written and designed with the student in mind. Links to free interactive study aids, like **Gimme-An-A,** help you prepare for exams, take course quizzes, and boost your understanding of key course concepts. Our Students tab also offers easy access to online **Career Resources,** including job listings and résumé tips.

Not only have we created a page that provides links to tools and valuable study material, you can also search for important information regarding your course's appropriate textbook via **Find A Subject/Book Site.**

Within each discipline, or area of study, you will find more detailed information regarding the textbook.

INTRODUCTION TO ECONOMICS TOPICS

The Thomson Learning Publishers Economics Website (http://www.swcollege.com/bef/economics.html) provides resources that help you:

- Understand your current course in Economics
- Learn about the academic and professional fields of Economics

Here is an overview of what you will find on the site:

- FIND YOUR TEXTBOOK! Click on the "By Course" icon, to find information and support resources associated with the book you are currently using, books you will use in other courses, and additional course-related material in the following areas:

- Comparative Economic Systems
- E-Commerce
- Econometrics / Forecasting
- Economic History
- Economic Thought
- Economics of Poverty / Inequality / Discrimination
- Environmental Economics
- Government & Business / Antitrust
- Health Economics
- Industrial Organization
- Intermediate Macroeconomics
- Intermediate Microeconomics / Price Theory
- International Economics
- Introductory Economics / Economic Issues (non-majors)
- Labor Economics
- Managerial Economics
- Mathematical Economics
- Microeconomic Theory
- Money and Banking
- Pre-MBA
- Principles of Economics (one term)
- Principles of Economics (two terms)
- Principles of Economics Course Enhancements
- Principles of Macroeconomics
- Principles of Microeconomics
- Public Finance

✦ RESOURCE CENTER. Click on the following links on the "How may we help you?" drop-down menu for Students to find additional Economics resources:

- VISIT THE STUDENT CENTER: Explore information about careers in Economics, and check out links to online Economics resources.

- ANSWER YOUR QUESTIONS (FAQs): Find more information about your Economics textbook and other Thomson Learning – South-Western products.
- MAKE ECONOMICS YOUR CAREER: Explore graduate school and professional opportunities in Economics.
- READ OUR ANNOUNCEMENTS: Check out the latest resources available from Thomson Learning.

PART III

Economics Websites

HITS Hottest Economics Sites on the Web

Introduction and General Material

Instructional Resources

Current Events

Economic Research and Analysis

Tutorials Online

Academic Integrity

General Research Information

Economic Journals and Working Papers

Data – U.S. Sources

International Data

Search Engines

Software

Careers in Economics

Economics Humor and Fun

HITS Hottest Economics Sites on the Web

Introduction and General Material

To aid navigation through these pages we tried to fit each of the sites into a specific category. While some sites fit nicely into a particular section, others could have been placed in several different sections. With this overlap in material you will want to consider our entire list when searching for a particular topic or Website.

Bill Geoffe's Resources for Economists on the Internet (RFE)

The main academic site for economists on the Web in the United States is Bill Geoffe's Resources for Economists on the Internet (RFE). From the front page you can select a general category and then go directly to the site, or to a description by Geoffe. The page is frequently updated. It is a good first place to go for research projects.

http://www.rfe.org/

and mirrored (meaning there's an identical copy) at:

http://coba.shsu.edu/EconFAQ/EconFAQ.html

RFE is one of two sites that make up the Economics Virtual Library. The homepage of the Virtual Library is:

http://www.hkkk.fi/EconVLib.html

and the WebEc page (representing most of the European and Japanese sites, and the other half of the Virtual Library) can be found at:

http://www.helsinki.fi/WebEc/

INSTRUCTIONAL RESOURCES

Resources for Economists on the Internet

An excellent source of information on teaching related activities. This includes classroom games, course packets, syllabi, software, distance learning resources, glossary of research terms, tutorials and online exercises, and much more.

http://www.rfe.org/Teaching/index.html

Dismal Scientist

A good opening site for economics students as well is the Dismal Scientist (from the term "dismal science" given to economics by Thomas Malthus).

http://www.dismal.com

ECONlinks

Scott Simkins operates ECONlinks, a front page for students in economics and business. The list of links is purposely not encyclopedic, but contains a variety of resources that you will find useful in your courses.

http://www.ncat.edu/~simkinss/econlinks.html

RationalExpectations.com

Ralph Lazar has created a relatively new site called RationalExpectations.com, which is meant to be a "resource for anyone interested in [emerging markets] economics — students, teachers, lecturers, journalists, professionals, or just the curious."

http://www.rationalexpectations.com/

EconomicsSearch.com

There is also EconomicsSearch.com. which intends to be a "one-stop shopping site specifically designed for economists and students of economics." It has a search engine for data and research papers that organizes materials by topic. It also provides a job service and information on graduate schools, as well as some study guides and tutorials.

http://www.economicsearch.com/

Scout Report for Business and Economics

If you want to see what is new on the Web in economics and business, the Scout Report for Business and Economics publishes a page every two weeks. Its staff of librarians and area specialists comb the Web looking for new sites, and provide descriptions of them.

http://scout.cs.wisc.edu/report/bus-econ/current/index.html

Ed Yardeni's Economics Network

One site that blends data and analysis is Ed Yardeni's Economics Network, a site chock-a-block with graphs and charts, and some analysis included. Some of it is protected for his clients. Yardeni is chief economist at the bank Deutsche Bank Securities.

http://www.205.232.265.149/

Global Macroeconomics and Financial Policy

Another excellent site is the Global Macroeconomics and Financial Policy Site provided by Nouriel Roubini of New York University. It provides a wide variety of research, news and data.

http://www.stern.nyu.edu/globalmacro/

About.com

John Irons is the guide for the about.com economics page. "About.com" creates subject-oriented sites with an expert subject guide. This page is the one for economics and finance.

http://economics.about.com/finance/economics/

Ron Davies

Interested in the history of money? Ron Davies has put a book online that provides an excellent tracing of the history of money from ancient times to present.

http://www.ex.ac.uk/~RDavies/arian/llyfr.html

Currencies of the World

Ronnie J. Phillips presents the Currencies of the World. Here you will find an impressive collection of images of currency used throughout U.S. history as well as those used throughout the world.

http://lamar.colostate.edu/~rphillip/currency.html

Adam Smith

You have probably learned that the first writer of modern economics was Adam Smith. You can learn more about him here.

http://www.efr.hw.ac.uk/EDC/edinburghers/adam-smith.html

Wealth of Nations

Alternatively, you could read the entire text of *Wealth of Nations* online here.

http://socserv2.socsci.mcmaster.ca/~econ/ugcm/3ll3/smith/wealth/index.html

Nobel Prize in Economics Winners

The winners of the Nobel Prize in Economics can be found here.

http://www.nobel.se/economics/laureates/index.html

CURRENT EVENTS

Students of economics should try to read some business and economics news daily. There are many sites that can do this, but here's three that are national in scope and widely popular.

The Wall Street Journal

http://www.wsj.com

Investors' Business Daily

http://www.investors.com/

CNNfn, the financial network arm of CNN

http://cnnfn.cnn.com/

Bloomberg Online

http://www.bloomberg.com

Those wanting a more international focus should consider these sources:

Financial Times

http://www.ft.com

the US version is at:

http://www.usa.ft.com

The Economist

http://www.economist.com

Asian Wall Street Journal

http://interactive.wsj.com/asian/p/asiahome.html

The Far Eastern Economic Review

http://www.feer.com/

Wall Street Journal Europe

http://interactive.wsj.com/european/p/eurohome.html

Economic Research and Analysis

Increasingly, there are companies providing economic research and analysis to current events. These can be used in addition to the pages above to flesh out, for example, a paper on some current issues in economics.

Data Resources Incorporated (DRI)

One example of economic research and analysis to current events is Data Resources Incorporated (DRI), a longstanding forecasting firm in the U.S.

http://www.dri-wefa.com/main.cfm

Analysis from FirstUnion Bank

http://www.firstunion.com/library/econews/

Morgan Stanley Dean Witter

You can get a more international view from the economists at Morgan Stanley Dean Witter (you have to register for this service, but registration is free and easy.)

http://www.msdw.com

Policy.com

This site has issues pages for many issues in politics and economics. It draws on Web-published material from think tanks and advocacy groups around the world. The material is organized by subject, making it an ideal first stop for a term paper on some current economic problem.

http://www.speakout.com/activism/news/

The National Bureau of Economic Research

This site has been the source of information on business cycle activity for over half a century. It also maintains some historical data series and sponsors a broad range of economic research.

http://www.nber.org

Polyconomics

An interesting site to visit is Polyconomics. The principal there, Jude Wanniski, was one of the three people reportedly present at the birth of supply-side economics (along with Arthur Laffer and Jack Kemp.) He gives lessons in his Supply-Side University. See also his Memo on the Margin (which is on the home page).

http://www.polyconomics.com

Supply-Side University:
http://www.polyconomics.com/univ.html

Paul Krugman's Current Events

Paul Krugman is an economist at MIT, and writes for *The New York Times, Fortune,* and *Slate* (an online magazine, http://www.slate.com). He has collected most of his writings on current events on his own page; the complexity of the articles varies, but he notes which are technical and which are not.

http://web.mit.edu/krugman/www/

Brad De Long

Brad De Long runs another such site at the University of California at Berkeley. You can find his papers and musings, as well as a book on economic history here.

http://www.j-bradford-delong.net/

Tutorials Online

Byron Brown's Microeconomic Spreadsheets

Byron Brown has put up a set of Excel spreadsheets that teach many of the microeconomic principles. He states that you need Netscape Navigator to load these and run them.

http://www.bus.msu.edu/econ/brown/pim/

Syracuse University

Do you need to brush up your math skills for principles or intermediate theory? A few professors at Syracuse would like to help you.

http://syllabus.syr.edu/cid/graph/book.html

John Pezzullo's Interactive Statistical Calculations

John Pezzullo's pages provide a full collection of Web-based statistical calculators (largely running Java) that you can use. These run the gamut from a simple mean and standard deviation to a full econometric program like SHAZAM. Some instruction is provided as well.

http://members.aol.com/johnp71/javastat.html

Excel Spreadsheets

Excel can be used as well in economics. Here's a site that provides spreadsheets for cost analysis, elasticity, and profit maximization. You'll need Excel 97 or 2000 to run these spreadsheets.

http://www.bized.ac.uk/stafsup/options/sheets/econ_index.htm

AMOSweb

You can find a glossary of terms in economics at AMOSweb (see more about this in the humor section below).

http://www.amosweb.com/gls/

FACSNET

FACSNET provides another glossary. Terms are organized alphabetically, and you can click down to the first letter of the term you want.

http://www.facsnet.org/tools/ref_tutor/econo_term/glossary.html

ACADEMIC INTEGRITY

Academic Honesty

A number of sites have emerged to fight an unfortunate aspect of the expansion of the Web — the rise of plagiarism. These sites include organizations devoted to academic honesty and guides to many plagiarism topics.

http://www.academicintegrity.org/

http://www.csuohio.edu/a_and_s/faculty/handbook/genint/plagweb.htm

The following are programs to detect plagiarism:

EVE

http://www.canexus.com/eve/index.shtml

IntegriGuard

http://ww w.integriguard.com/

Plagiarism.org

http://www.plagiarism.org/

General Research Information

American Economic Association

http://www.aeaweb.org

Committee on the Status of Women in the Economics Profession (CSWEP)

http://www.cswep.org/

Job Openings for Economists

http://www.eco.utexas.edu/joe/

U.S. and Foreign Economics Departments

http://www.amosweb.com/econdept/

Christian Zimmerman's Links to Economics Departments

Christian Zimmerman has gathered together the Web pages of over 5,000 economics departments and institutes in over 190 countries in one place. You can search by country, name or areas. There's a quick link to U.S. departments.

http://ideas.uqam.ca/EDIRC/index.html

Economic Journals and Working Papers

JSTOR

JSTOR is a archive for scholarly journals:

http://www.jstor.org/jstor/

Many Economic journals have Web pages that provide information on submitting a manuscript, details on forthcoming articles, abstracts, etc.

Economic Journals on the Web

http://www.oswego.edu/~economic/journals.htm

EconLit

http://www.econlit.org/econlit/ellistjn.html

WebEc — Economics Journals on the Internet

http://www.helsinki.fi/WebEc/journals.html

Journal of Economic Literature Classification System

Below is a page that provides the details of the *Journal of Economic Literature Classification System* for manuscripts and books.

http://econwpa.wustl.edu/explajelfine.html

EconPapers

EconPapers provides access to RePEc, the world's largest collection of online Economics working papers, journal articles and software.

http://econpapers.hhs.se/

Other working paper sites include:

Center for Economic Policy Research

http://www.cepr.org/pubs/new-dps/dplist.asp

National Bureau of Economic Research

http://papers.nber.org/papers.html

DATA – U.S. SOURCES

U.S. Federal Reserve Bank

Below you will find a set of links to every U.S. Federal Reserve Bank. At each of these you can find national and regional data, working papers and publications. Many are quite readable for undergraduate students in economics.

The Board of Governors of the Federal Reserve System

http://www.federalreserve.gov/

Federal Reserve Bank of Atlanta

http://www.frbatlanta.org/

Federal Reserve Bank of Boston

http://www.std.com/frbbos/

Federal Reserve Bank of Chicago

http://www.chicagofed.org/

Federal Reserve Bank of Cleveland

http://www.clev.frb.org/

Federal Reserve Bank of Dallas

http://www.dallasfed.org/

Federal Reserve Bank of Kansas City

http://www.kc.frb.org/

Federal Reserve Bank of Minneapolis

http://woodrow.mpls.frb.fed.us/

Federal Reserve Bank of New York

http://www.ny.frb.org/

Federal Reserve Bank of Philadelphia

http://www.phil.frb.org/

Federal Reserve Bank of Richmond

http://www.rich.frb.org/

Federal Reserve Bank of St. Louis

http://www.stls.frb.org/

Federal Reserve Bank of San Francisco

http://www.frbsf.org/

FRED®

A particularly excellent source for aggregate macroeconomic data is found at FRED®, the Economic Time-Series Database provided by Federal Reserve Bank of St. Louis.

http://www.stls.frb.org/fred/

The three main pieces of data used to measure a macroeconomy are gross domestic product, inflation and unemployment. The Commerce Department releases data on GDP, while the Labor Department releases information on the consumer price index and unemployment. Most of the data is gathered together in simple pages, with links to any background or historical information you might want.

GDP

http://www.bea.doc.gov/briefrm/gdp.htm

CPI

http://www.bls.gov/cpi/

Unemployment

http://www.bls.gov/cps/

Aggregate and state-level macro- and microeconomic data series are available at:

Banking Data and Research

http://www.ala.org/acrl/resnov99.html

Bureau of Labor Statistics

http://www.bls.gov/

Bureau of Economic Analysis

http://www.bea.doc.gov/

Bureau of Economic Analysis Regional Accounts

http://www.bea.doc.gov/bea/regional/data.htm

Department of Commerce

http://home.doc.gov/

Department of the Treasury

http://www.ustreas.gov/

National Longitudinal Surveys

http://www.chrr.ohio-state.edu/nls-bib/

National Science Foundation

http://www.nsf.gov/

Panel Study on Income Dynamics

http://www.isr.umich.edu/src/psid/

Social Security Administration

http://www.ssa.gov/

Statistical Abstract of the U.S.

http://www.census.gov/prod/www/statistical-abstract-us.html

U.S. Census Bureau

http://www.census.gov

The White House

The White House provides the Economics Statistics Briefing Room as a simple site to see some basic economic data. Links are provided to other government sites for more information.

http://www.whitehouse.gov/fsbr/esbr.html

Index of Leading Economic Indicators

The Conference Board publishes the *Index of Leading Economic Indicators,* the index of help-wanted advertising and a consumer confidence survey. All of these are useful in predicting what will happen to the economy in the near future.

http://www.tcb-indicators.org/

Congressional Budget Office (CBO)

For current federal spending and revenue as well as macro forecasts, consult the Congressional Budget Office (CBO).

http://www.cbo.gov/

University of Michigan's Survey of Consumers

For an established survey of consumer attitudes, consult the University of Michigan's Survey of Consumers:

http://athena.sca.isr.umich.edu

EconoMagic

Ted Bos operates EconoMagic, a Website that collects national economic data from a number of sources. The data can be downloaded directly into spreadsheets; one can use the site to generate graphs of the data as well.

http://www.economagic.com

Dryden Press

Dryden Press also maintains a quick snapshot view of state of the U.S. economy, with links to charts and source press releases linked by EconoMagic.

http://www.harcourtcollege.com/econ/state.html

INTERNATIONAL DATA

The Central Bank Resource

Mark Bernkopf is Webmaster for The Central Bank Resource page, a site that provides links to a great many central banks' and finance ministries' Web resources around the world.

http://patriot.net/~bernkopf/

Internationally, the International Monetary Fund and the World Bank are very important institutions. They also provide a large amount of data and research about other economies. Most of their material is free.

The International Monetary Fund

http://www.imf.org

The World Bank

http://www.worldbank.org

The World Bank has organized its burgeoning research on economic growth into a separate page.

http://www.worldbank.org/research/growth/

The Pacific Exchange Rate Service

The Pacific Exchange Rate Service provides current and historical information on exchange rates for over 100 countries.

http://pacific.commerce.ubc.ca/xr/

Penn World Tables

One problem with most economic data internationally is the lack of comparability. The World Bank has sponsored the Penn World Tables, a set of data for over 150 countries that is comparable. Those doing international economics will want to use this resource.

http://datacentre2.chass.utoronto.ca/pwt/

The CIA

The CIA keeps a set of data online that provides information on every country it studies. These studies make excellent starting points for research on a different country, should you be asked to study one by your professor.

http://www.odci.gov/cia/publications/factbook/index.html

U.S. State Department

You can learn about their trade with the U.S. from the U.S. State Department's country reports on economic policy and trade practices.

http://www.state.gov/www/issues/economic/trade_reports/

SEARCH ENGINES

Data on the Net

Data on the Net surveys 400 social science sites.
http://odwin.ucsd.edu/idata/

FEDSTATS

This site searches pages from over 70 different federal agencies.
http://www.fedstats.gov/

Federal Web Locator

Federal Web Locator provides a directory for federal government sites.
http://www.infoctr.edu/fwl/

FirstGov

FirstGov is a federal government search site.
http://Firstgov.gov/

SOFTWARE

Estima (RATS)

http://www.estima.com

Guide to Available Mathematical Software (GAMS)

http://gams.nist.gov/

LaTeX / MikTeX

Freeware Windows LaTeX program (MikTeX):
http://www.miktex.org

Shareware Windows LaTeX Editor (WinEdt):
http://www.winedt.com/

Mathematica
http://www.wri.com

Matlab
http://www.matlab.com

Jim LeSage's MATLAB Econometrics Function Library
http://www.spatial-econometrics.com/

Stata Corporation
http://www.stata.com

Statistical Software Component Archive
http://ideas.uqam.ca/ideas/data/bocbocode.html

Stata Tutorial
http://www.oac.ucla.edu/training/stata/

StataList Archives
http://www.egroups.com

GAUSS Software Archive
http://gurukul.ucc.american.edu/econ/gaussres/gaussidx.htm

CAREERS IN ECONOMICS

Economists' Salaries
Economists are paid well, as you can see on this graph.
http://www.census.gov/ftp/pub/hhes/www/img/edugraph.html

Careers

The kinds of jobs you can get with a bachelor's degree is well explained in this piece as well.

http://ball.econ.vt.edu/Careers/KindsJobs.html

Job Openings for Economists

But where to get them? The American Economics Association provides a job openings publication to its members called *Job Openings for Economists.* Most of these are academic, but the last section contains non-academic jobs. It is worth viewing to see what kinds of opportunities might await a career in economics.

http://www.eco.utexas.edu/joe/

National Association of Business Economics

The National Association of Business Economists provides a Website that describes its activities. Many business and government economists are members of this organization. You have to join for complete access, which would include job openings and a membership directory.

http://www.nabe.com/

Ph.D. Programs in the U.S. and Canada

If you would like to consider graduate education in economics, you can visit SUNY-Albany's site with links to many Ph.D. program in the U.S. and Canada. There are some extra links at the bottom of the page to other lists as well.

http://www.albany.edu/econ/eco_phds.html

Omicron Delta Epsilon

Last, if you have done well in your studies in economics, you might be able to join Omicron Delta Epsilon, the honor society in economics. You can read about them and see if there's a chapter in your university here.

http://www.cba.ua.edu/~ode/visitors.htm

Economics Humor and Fun

The JokEc

I suppose you think we don't have any, but we do. The JokEc page is an excellent place to go for jokes about economists and economics. If you get more than half of these jokes, you must really understand economics!

http://netec.wustl.edu/JokEc.html

AMOSweb

Orley Amos, a professor at Oklahoma State University, runs AMOSweb as economics with a touch of whimsy. The whimsy is most apparent on his page "Ask Mister Economy." You can find things slightly more serious elsewhere on AMOSweb.

http://www.amosweb.com/ame/

"Where's George?"

This is both fun and educational: "Where's George?" — the site where people keep track of the movement of dollar bills, is useful for the study of the velocity of currency as well as entertaining for the posts included with the times and places of the dollars.

http://www.wheresgeorge.com

Budgetary Decisions Game

Think you can run an economy? Here's a game that allows you to make budgetary decisions about the U.S. economy and observe their effects.

http://garnet.berkeley.edu:3333/budget/budget-1.html

Iowa Electronic Market

You probably think by now that economists will put a price on anything. Well, maybe so. You can trade futures in political contests, Microsoft's stock price, or something more at the Iowa Electronic Market. Participants buy and sell futures online with real money.

http://www.biz.uiowa.edu/iem/

APPENDIX

INFOTRAC®
COLLEGE EDITION

QUICK START GUIDE

This guide will assist you in reaching your academic potential through the use of INFOTRAC College Edition.*

* Not every institution and every instructor participates in the InfoTrac program. For those of you who are participants, please use the following pages as a quick start guide to the service.

INFOTRAC® COLLEGE EDITION

Quick Start Guide

InfoTrac College Edition is a fully searchable online university library containing complete articles and their images. Its database gives you access to hundreds of scholarly and popular publications — including magazines, journals, encyclopedias, and newsletters. Updated daily, the *InfoTrac College Edition* database also includes articles dating back as much as four years. And every article within the database can be easily printed for reading and reference purposes or quickly arranged into a bibliography.

Start Here

Go to

http://www.infotrac-college.com/

Click

Enter *InfoTrac College*

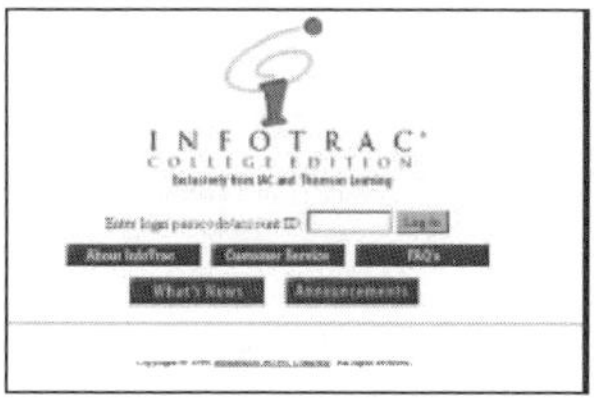

Enter your passcode.

*(Hang on to your passcode.
You will need it every time you log in.)*

First time using *InfoTrac College Edition?*

To learn how to activate your account, turn to Page A-4.

Looking for articles?

For hints on searching, turn to Pages A-5 through A-8.

ACTIVATING YOUR ACCOUNT

If you are using *InfoTrac College Edition* for the first time, you will need to complete the registration form. Any items in **bold** type must be completed before your account can be activated. *(see Figure 1)*

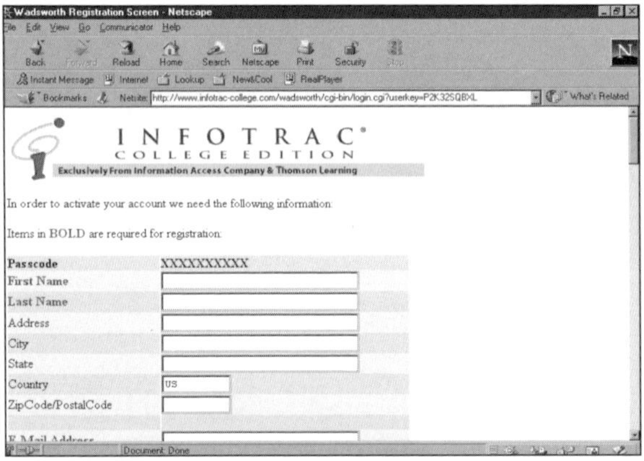

Figure 1.
Registration Screen

If required items are missing or invalid on the registration form, an error message from Customer Service describing the problem will appear. Simply click the "Back" button on your browser's toolbar to return to the registration form. *(see Figure 2)*

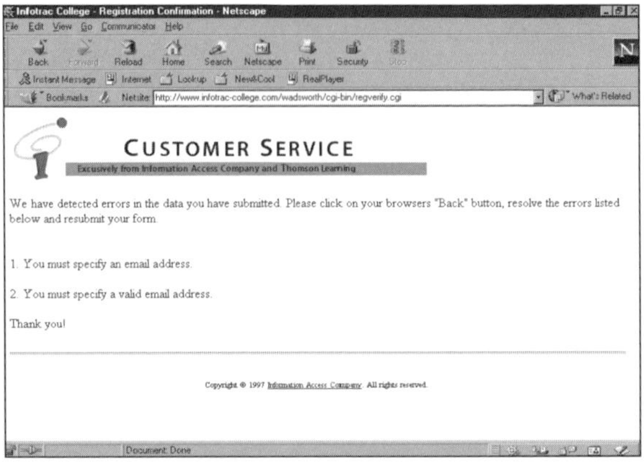

Figure 2.
Error Message

After the registration form is successfully completed, you will be asked to confirm that all information is accurate. Click on the "Submit" button to send in your completed registration form. (see Figure 3)

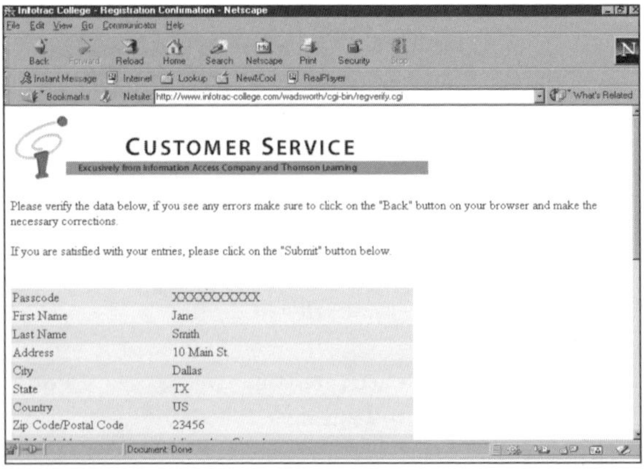

Figure 3.
Confirmation Screen

SEARCHING THE *INFOTRAC* *COLLEGE EDITION* DATABASE

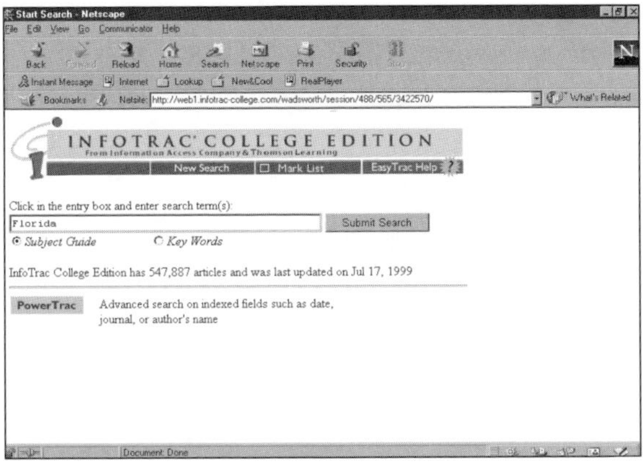

After signing in, the search screen will appear. Type in the topic you would like to research. Select "Subject Guide" or "Key Words" and click the "Submit Search" button. *(see Figure 4)*

Figure 4.
Search Screen

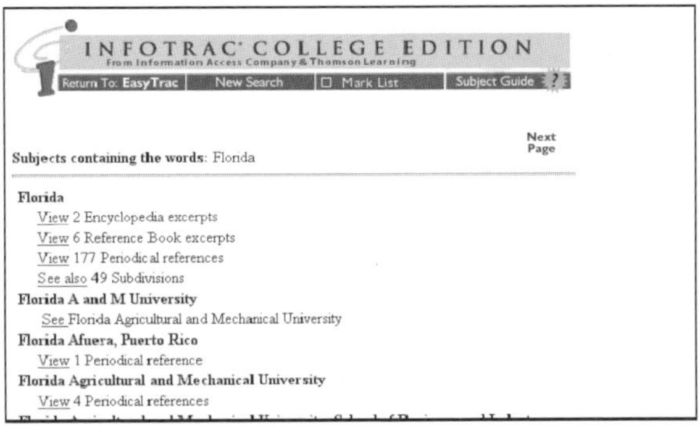

Figure 5.
Subject Screen

Subject Guide Search

If you search words that do not match the Subject Guide database, a list of similar and related subjects will come up on the screen. Simply select the subject that most closely matches your topic.

Once a subject has been selected from the database, a screen will appear with links to Periodical References, Subdivisions, and Related Subjects. *(see Figure 5)*

Periodical References will list the title, author and publications for articles available on your subject.

Subdivisions will list subcategories of articles in your subject.

Related Subjects will list topics closely associated to your subject.

continued . . .

SEARCHING THE *INFOTRAC* *COLLEGE EDITION* DATABASE, *continued*

A list will appear on the screen containing bibliographic information for each article in your search to a maximum of 20 articles per page. *(see Figure 6)*

To select an article, check the "Mark" box by clicking on it with your mouse.

To read your selected articles, click on the "View text and retrieval choices" link.

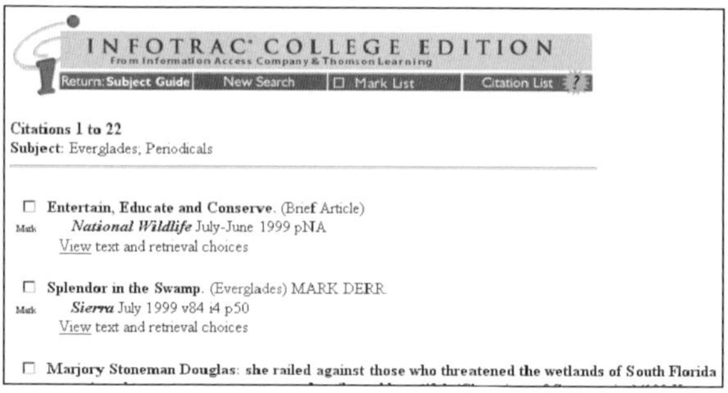

Figure 6.
List of Articles

Your marked articles will have the bibliographic information at the top of the article followed by an abstract (when available) and the full text of the article. To browse through your articles, click on the Prev. << Record >> Next link. Articles can also be printed. *(see Figure 7)*

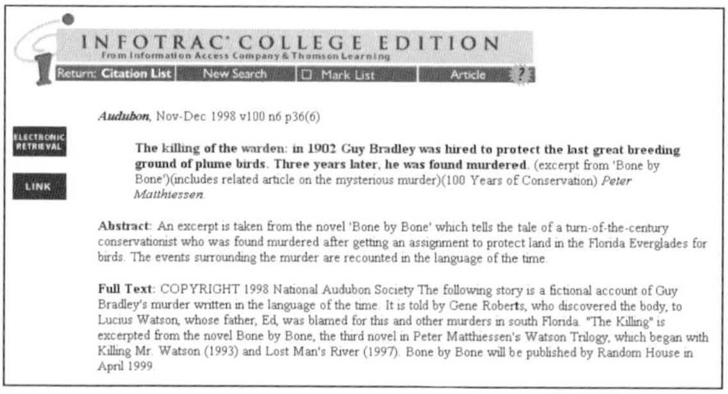

Figure 7.
Sample Article

With PowerTrac, a more complex search can be conducted. Click on the ▼ on the "Select an Index" listbox, choose the type of criteria you want to search for. The code for your criteria will appear in the entry box. Type your criteria in the entry box after the code. *(see Figure 8)*

If you want to search by multiple criterion, simply repeat the process with an operator between them (see list below).

Logical operators (and/or/not) specify inclusive or exclusive relationships between search terms or result sets.

continued . . .

SEARCHING THE *INFOTRAC* *COLLEGE EDITION* DATABASE, *continued*

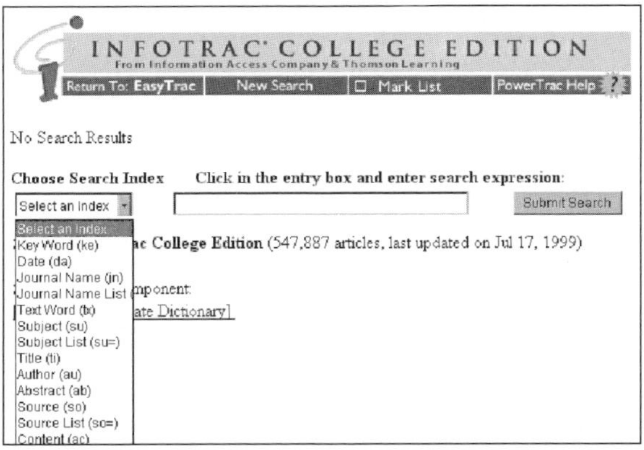

Figure 8.
PowerTrac Search Screen

Proximity operators (Wn,Nn) specify that two search terms must be within a specified distance (in words) of each other. Proximity operators work only with free text indexes such as keywords, abstracts, text, and titles.

Range operators (since, before, etc.) specify upper bounds, lower bounds, or both in searches for numeric data. Numeric indexes include publication dates, number of employees, and annual sales.

Nesting operators determine the order in which operators are evaluated.

Indexes for Searching in PowerTrac

Abstract (ab): Includes words from article abstracts as well as from any author's abstracts.

Author (au): Authors are indexed in surname/given name order, for example, "Nelan bruce w." It's best to search in surname-first order. Enter a surname and, optionally, a given name.

Content (ac): Lets you locate all records with full text and eliminate those without. To search this index, enter the word "fulltext."

Date (da): The date the article was published.

Journal Name (jn): The name of the magazine or periodical.

Journal Name List (jn=): Provides a list of magazines or periodicals in which the search topic appears.

Key Word (ke): Words in article titles and authors, as well as subjects, people, companies, products, vocations, events, etc., featured in articles.

continued . . .

SEARCHING THE *INFOTRAC* COLLEGE EDITION DATABASE, *continued*

Record Number (rn): A full record always includes a unique record number. If you note a record number, you can easily find the record again with the record number index.

Source (so): Lets you search for records by the source from which they're taken (e.g., encyclopedia or newsletter).

Source List (so=): Lets you browse an alphabetical list of subjects that contain the word or words you type.

Subject (su): Lets you search for references by the topic under which they are indexed.

Subject List (su=): Provides a list of references by topic.

Text Word (tx): Composed of words from the body of articles and reports.

Title (ti): The title index is composed of all words in article, report, or book titles.

Using Wildcards in PowerTrac Searches

At times, you might want to find more than just exact matches to a search term. For instance, you might want to find both the singular and plural forms of a word or variant spellings. Wildcards let you broaden your searches to match a pattern.

InfoTrac provides three wildcards:

- An asterisk (*) stands for any number of characters, including none. For example, **pigment*** matches "pigment," "pigments," "pigmentation," etc.
- A question mark (?) stands for exactly one character. Multiple question marks in a row stand for the same number of characters as there are question marks. For example, **psych????y** matches either "psychology" or "psychiatry" but not "psychotherapy."
- An exclamation point (!) stands for one or no characters. For example, **analog!!** matches "analog," "analogs" or "analogue" but not "analogous."

If you see a message about a search being invalid, you'll need to add at least one character before one of the wildcards.

Professor Name ______________________________

Course Name ______________________________

Course Number ______________________________